"This book is a wonderful reminder of the importance of the biblical text not only for a seminary curriculum, but also for all its environment. Well chosen articles from a theological giant who will satisfy scholars as well as those church leaders looking for a solid basis for theological education. A must read!"
— **Gerardo A. Alfaro**, Professor of Theological Studies, Director of Spanish Program, Dallas Theological Seminary

"Rowan Williams once said that we do not know where our debts end, theologically speaking. I agree. But I at least know I am indebted beyond measure to the two men who have edited this volume, Jason Lee and Ched Spellman, and the man whose teaching ministry they have faithfully stewarded, John Sailhamer. Coming to grips with understanding the words of Scripture as the locus of God's revelation, and all the implications that come with it, along with reckoning with the canonical order of the Scriptures as an interpretive guide changed my life. And all of this occurred within a textual community that left an indelible mark on my understanding of hermeneutics and theological education. To Dr. Lee, Dr. Spellman, and Dr. Sailhamer, I say thank you for teaching me the fullness of what it means to "take up and read" the Scriptures as God's very word to us and for us, and our salvation."
— **Zachary M. Bowden**, Assistant Professor of Theological Studies, Cedarville University

"As one of those who had the privilege of learning from Dr. Sailhamer not only through his better-known publications but also in the classroom and in informal settings, I know firsthand the wealth of knowledge and wisdom that his brilliant mind had to offer. Spellman and Lee have done us a service by making available for a broader audience Sailhamer's vision for theological education (along with their own reflections on it), which powerfully emphasizes the centrality of Scripture, breaks down the distinction between the "theoretical" and the "practical," and insists on the seminary as a community in its own right, even as it exists for the church. The additional carefully-selected pieces concerning the relationship between hermeneutics and history provide theological underpinnings for this vision and are a convenient collection of Sailhamer's thinking on this important topic."
— **Kevin Chen**, Associate Professor of Old Testament, Christian Witness Theological Seminary

"John Sailhamer was a brilliant Old Testament scholar who faithfully served both Baptist and evangelical institutions during his lifetime. In this new volume, edited by Jason Lee and Ched Spellman, readers are introduced to Sailhamer's fully-orbed vision for a scripturally-grounded understanding of theological education. In a day when seminaries and divinity schools are pulled in multiple directions from both churches and culture, from social issues and pragmatic concerns, this thoughtfully developed volume points readers toward a model for renewal for theological education by connecting teaching, learning, and practice to the biblical text in a fresh, winsome, and coherent manner. I am happy to recommend *The Seminary as Textual Community* as an important resource for administrators, board members, and faculty, as well as pastors and denominational leaders."

— **David S. Dockery**, President, International Alliance for Christian Education; Distinguished Professor of Theology, Southwestern Baptist Theological Seminary

"John Sailhamer has always appeared gigantic to me. From my student days in proximity to him at Southeastern Seminary, to days accessing him at a distance through his writing, his stature remained fixed and large. His largeness is due not only to his reputation as a scholar, but also, and more so, due to his love of the Bible. Thus, I was delighted to see this new volume that adds to the Sailhamer legendarium, and of import, on the topic of theological education. Like with much of Sailhamer's work, there is a refreshing simplicity that makes *The Seminary as a Textual Community* profound. Seminaries should serve churches and they do so best by equipping students to treasure the Bible and seeing the Bible the central text for study. Thanks to Ched Spellman and Jason K. Lee for bringing Sailhamer the Giant back into view for the good of us all."

— **Jason G. Duesing**, Provost and Senior Vice President for Academic Administration, Professor of Historical Theology, Midwestern Seminary and Spurgeon College

"*The Seminary as a Textual Community* summons a new generation of theologians and church leaders to wrestle with John Sailhamer's vision for theological education and provides context for why his approach stands out from so many others. It applies Sailhamer's commitment to the biblical text and hermeneutics to the task of forming "textual communities" that yield gospel ministry. His approach challenges all theological educators to consider if we truly rely on God's Word. For those of us who have known Sailhamer's work, this volume reminds us of how his scholarship answers one of our most pressing problems: teaching God's eternal truths to the next generation. Of course, for those who have not yet engaged with his ideas, this volume introduces them to a needed conversation and places them within a growing community of those indebted to God's work in John Sailhamer's life."

— **Peter Link**, Chair and Associate Professor of Christian Studies, Charleston Southern University

"Through the years of my own teaching vocation, I've become convinced that creative teaching doesn't begin with the methods we use, but with fresh, creative approaches to the subjects we teach. We often assume that the questions traditionally asked, and the answers given, are the "right" ones. Looking back, the most effective model for me of creative, respectful questioning of the questions was John Sailhamer, both in the classes I took and the private discussions I had with him. This book explains not just the "how" of biblical and theological education, but the "why." The fact that his own teaching has now had paradigm-changing impact on several generations of his students verifies that John was a master teacher and discipler, as you see in the reflections in this volume."

— **Ray Lubeck**, Professor, Multnomah University

"Dietrich Bonhoeffer believed that proper seminary training for the sake of healthy local church ministry must take place in a setting where students can enjoy and practice 'life together.' This community existed only through and in Jesus Christ under the Word. To add, OT scholar John Sailhamer offers a robust and exciting vision for seminary as a distinct textual community, one whose 'common life' is entirely shaped and constituted by the written Word of God, the Holy Scriptures. In an age where challenges to 'visible, communal' ministry education and training abound, Spellman and Lee have given the rest of us a special gift by making accessible Sailhamer's paradigm-shifting essay on a 'theological seminary.' Alongside other demonstrations of Sailhamer's text-oriented approach to Scripture exercised across the disciplines, Spellman and Lee offer valued commentary and reflection upon the retrospect and prospect of Sailhamer's contribution to the world of theological education. May we heed these insights so that 'seminary life' will rightly exist in and through the living Word, Jesus Christ, who is known in the written Word, Holy Scripture, and in this way, truly be for the sake of God's church."

— **William M. Marsh**, Assistant Professor of Theology, Director, MDiv Program, Cedarville, University

"This book's driving force is the conviction that the Christian seminary, as a part of the Christian Church, is fundamentally a hermeneutical entity; its identity is found in the Bible as written text, and its purpose and task are directed towards discipleship in God's word. In *The Seminary as A Textual Community*, Ched Spellman and Jason K. Lee compile and reflect upon a previously-unpublished address of Sailhamer's, along with a handful of his other related publications, to present a book that will be of great benefit to many. Biblical scholars and theologians, pastors, and any student of the Bible will glean from its theological and hermeneutical reflections. And the practical suggestions for curricular design and pedagogy will guide seminary administrative leadership and faculty as well. This is a trove of valuable insight."

— **Josh Matthews**, Assistant Professor of Biblical Studies, Chair, Center for Biblical and Theological Studies, Western Seminary

"True to his normal practice, John Sailhamer probes a wide array of German and early modern scholars in order to propose a comprehensive foundation for seminary education. Editors Lee and Spellman situate Sailhamer's proposal in the midst of Sailhamer's academic work as well as his evangelical context. In their own summary, they highlight some of Sailhamer's contributions for the everchanging effort in structuring a seminary education and offer additional works by Sailhamer that non-specialists can engage. Always wanting the Bible to have its say, Sailhamer gives evangelicals a great deal to think about in the way we organize and carry out our seminary task. If changing times has minimized our current effectiveness, perhaps we should listen to his proposal."

— **Tracy McKenzie**, Associate Professor of Old Testament and Hebrew, Southeastern Baptist Theological Seminary

"My first exposure to Sailhamer's essay came at a time when I was teaching at a seminary that was housed within a church building and had a close relationship with that ministry. Sailhamer's words were instrumental in casting a vision for the textual nature of my work there. Having sat under Sailhamer's text-centered teaching, this essay helped make the connection between the hermeneutical approach I had heard in the classroom and the seminary's existence "because of and in behalf of the Scriptures." This essay helped shape my thoughts about my own personal ministry, as such an expert in the field articulated clearly the implications of Christianity as "a religion of the Book." For years, discussions with colleagues about the nature of a "textual community" have been spurred on by thoughts in Sailhamer's essay. I cannot recommend this essay enough, and I am thankful for the work of Spellman and Lee to make it available to a larger audience."

— **Randall L. McKinion**, Professor of Old Testament, Cedarville University

"There are a few things this side of eternity I consider to be life's greatest treasures. One of my greatest treasures is being one of Dr. Sailhamer's last two PhD students. Dr. Sailhamer's scholarship and mentorship in and out of the classroom created an irresistible gravitational pull towards living (in the words of Thomas Mann) the "quoted life," which the Sailhamer defines as "a life that conceptualizes its own existence in terms of authoritative texts" (p. 10). A constant regret I've lived with the past 9 years serving as the academic dean of Israel College of the Bible is not having the ear and the guidance of my beloved mentor. "If only I could have asked Dr. Sailhamer about…" Spellman and Lee's new publication brought Dr. Sailhamer into my life once again (I write this with tears). Reading this book, it felt as though Dr. Sailhamer and I were sitting together in my living room in Israel for two exhilarating days as he provoked me to jealousy yet again. I was reminded and challenged by the vision of a text-centered theological education, an education which invites both faculty members and students alike to aspire to live the quoted life. I am deeply indebted and grateful to the editors for the publication of this amazing book, which is a must read for everyone who is called to serve in or be served in theological education."

— **Seth Postell**, Academic Dean, Israel College of the Bible

"John Sailhamer was a master teacher and model scholar. His classes and his example profoundly shaped my understanding of Scripture and my career as a student of Scripture. This volume accurately reflects Sailhamer's comprehensive and incisive understanding of theological education, hermeneutics, and the relationship of the biblical text to the events it narrates. This is a book that will provide fruitful insights for seminary administrators, theological faculty members and ministers across the whole ecclesiological spectrum. Spellman and Lee have selected, framed and introduced Sailhamer's distinctive contributions to the church and the seminary very well."

— **Mark Reasoner**, Professor of Biblical Theology, Marian University

"Spellman and Lee are to be commended for bringing to light John Sailhamer's previously unpublished piece, "The Nature, Purpose, and Tasks of a Theological Seminary," and for undergirding it with a careful selection of some of Sailhamer's lesser known articles and essays. As a former student of Dr. Sailhamer, I have personally benefited from his commitment to "teaching the written Word of God." His vision for theological education provides a much needed sense of priority and focus. My hope is that this book will help to unify seminary administrators, faculty, and students as "text communities" in the service of the local church."

— **Michael B. Shepherd**, Associate Professor of Biblical Studies, Cedarville University

"While it may not be as valuable as a hitherto unknown Beethoven work, the discovery of John Sailhamer's 1993 lecture on the nature and purpose of theological education is nevertheless cause for celebration, and equally symphonic, inasmuch as it gathers together the isolated instruments (read: departments) of a seminary into a unified orchestra: a textual community. Old and New Testament studies, church history, systematic and practical theology all share an interest in various aspects of biblical interpretation, be it making sense of the grammar of the text in its historical context, its reception down through the centuries, the coherence of its content, or its proclamation and ministry today. In fixing its curricular gaze with passion and clarity upon that integrative mission, Sailhamer's essay now appears ahead of its time. In this present moment, when theological higher education is in the midst of tectonic shifts, Sailhamer's proposal, and the essays that here accompany and elaborate it, deserve to be heard."

— **Kevin J. Vanhoozer**, Research Professor of Systematic Theology, Trinity Evangelical Divinity School

"This volume contributes by being an appropriate tribute to the late John Sailhamer. The tribute does not merely note his vast scholarly insight. It more profoundly highlights a theological vision through which Sailhamer served the church and called colleagues and students to do the same. Ched Spellman and Jason Lee have reverberated his influence by extending his text-focused vision. The timing is perfect. We are at the threshold of tremendous change in our social and cultural domains. The waves of the resulting disruption have only now begun to ripple. The task of ministry preparation in the service of the church will not be exempt from all of this commotion. In the midst of it all, we recognize that the church's calling remains intact , and faithfulness to it is as urgent as ever. And God's Word continues to stand as the illuminating Word through which we know him and know how to live in his world. That depends on faithful biblical interpretation. For Sailhamer, the reigning question related to biblical exegesis and theology was: "How do we go about finding what the biblical writers were teaching in their carefully wrought narratives?" Half of this book is dedicated to helping us see his hermeneutical approach for hearing the narrative of Scripture and seeing how the Scriptures are about the gospel. The book, though, is titled after Sailhamer's manifesto for seminary education. In it, he sets forth the conviction that for the church to remain a people of the Word, institutions who have as their mission to prepare ministers to serve the church must be above all 'textual communities.'"

— **Keith Whitfield**, Provost and Dean of Graduate Studies, Associate Professor of Theology, Southeastern Baptist Theological Seminary

"Reading the Bible—it sounds like such a simple idea. It was this simple idea to which John Sailhamer devoted his life. Sailhamer was one of the most insightful readers of the Bible, discovering thread upon thread of the Bible's coherent picture of the world through countless hours of reading the Bible. In this volume, Spellman and Lee present and reflect upon how Sailhamer's thoughts regarding reading the Bible influenced his thinking about biblical scholarship, theological education, and worldview formation. The volume provides a compelling vision for how reading the Bible with the proper questions can shape an academic discipline, a theological school, and an individual's view of the world. Such a delight to read and consider!"

— **Joshua E. Williams**, Associate Professor of Old Testament, Southwestern Baptist Theological Seminary

# The Seminary as a Textual Community

# The Seminary as a Textual Community: Exploring John Sailhamer's Vision for Theological Education

Ched Spellman & Jason K. Lee

Editors

Fontes

*The Seminary as a Textual Community:*
*Exploring John Sailhamer's Vision for Theological Education*

Copyright © 2021 by Ched Spellman and Jason K. Lee

ISBN-13: 978-1-948048-60-6

All rights reserved. No part of this publication may be reproduced, stored in a retrieval system, or transmitted in any form or by any means—electronic, mechanical, photocopy, recording, or any other—except for brief quotations in printed reviews, without the prior permission of the publisher.

FONTES PRESS

DALLAS, TX

www.fontespress.com

*Dedication:*
*For the family and students of John Sailhamer*

## Contents

PREFACE . . . . . . . . . . . . . . . . . . . . . . . . . . . . . . . . . . . . . . . . . . . . . . . . . . . . . . . xvii

FOREWORD: *Stephen G. Dempster* . . . . . . . . . . . . . . . . . . . . . . . . . . . . . . . . . . . xxi

1. THE NATURE, PURPOSE, AND TASKS OF A THEOLOGICAL SEMINARY . . . . . . 3
   1. The Seminary and the Christian Church . . . . . . . . . . . . . . . . . . . . . . . . . . 4
      *Excursus: Edward Farley's Theologia* . . . . . . . . . . . . . . . . . . . . . . . . . . . . 8
      *Summary* . . . . . . . . . . . . . . . . . . . . . . . . . . . . . . . . . . . . . . . . . . . . . . . . . . 9
   2. The Seminary and the Scriptures. . . . . . . . . . . . . . . . . . . . . . . . . . . . . . . 10
      *Summary* . . . . . . . . . . . . . . . . . . . . . . . . . . . . . . . . . . . . . . . . . . . . . . . . . .15
   3. The Seminary and the Academy . . . . . . . . . . . . . . . . . . . . . . . . . . . . . . . .15
      *Academia et Ecclesia* . . . . . . . . . . . . . . . . . . . . . . . . . . . . . . . . . . . . . . . . 16
      *The Function of the Seminary Text-Community within Academia* . . . .17
   Tasks and Disciplines . . . . . . . . . . . . . . . . . . . . . . . . . . . . . . . . . . . . . . . . . . . 26
   Tasks and Domains . . . . . . . . . . . . . . . . . . . . . . . . . . . . . . . . . . . . . . . . . . . . 26
   Domain 1: The Seminary Text-Community. . . . . . . . . . . . . . . . . . . . . . . . . 27
      *Levels of Skills—Scholarship.* . . . . . . . . . . . . . . . . . . . . . . . . . . . . . . . . . 30
      *Effects of Tasks and Skills* . . . . . . . . . . . . . . . . . . . . . . . . . . . . . . . . . . . .31
      *Implementation of Tasks 1 within a Seminary* . . . . . . . . . . . . . . . . . . . .31
      *Target Audience: The Seminary Community Itself?* . . . . . . . . . . . . . . . .31
      *Seminary Faculty Structure* . . . . . . . . . . . . . . . . . . . . . . . . . . . . . . . . . . 33
      *Seminary Curriculum Structure for Tasks 1* . . . . . . . . . . . . . . . . . . . . . . 34
      *The Effect of Curriculum Focus on the Seminary* . . . . . . . . . . . . . . . . . 34
      *Multiple Track ThM Curriculum.* . . . . . . . . . . . . . . . . . . . . . . . . . . . . . . 35
      *The Setting of Tasks 1* . . . . . . . . . . . . . . . . . . . . . . . . . . . . . . . . . . . . . . . 38
   Domain 2: The Seminary Text-Community within the
   Christian Church . . . . . . . . . . . . . . . . . . . . . . . . . . . . . . . . . . . . . . . . . . . . . 38
      *The Seminary and the Church.* . . . . . . . . . . . . . . . . . . . . . . . . . . . . . . . 38
      *Skills of Tasks 2 Applied to the Church* . . . . . . . . . . . . . . . . . . . . . . . . . 40
      *Implementation of Skills and Tasks* . . . . . . . . . . . . . . . . . . . . . . . . . . . . 40
      *Tasks 1 Links to Tasks 2* . . . . . . . . . . . . . . . . . . . . . . . . . . . . . . . . . . . . . 40
      *The Setting of Tasks 2* . . . . . . . . . . . . . . . . . . . . . . . . . . . . . . . . . . . . . . .41
   Domain 3: The Church within the World (Intersecting with
   Culture). . . . . . . . . . . . . . . . . . . . . . . . . . . . . . . . . . . . . . . . . . . . . . . . . . . . . 44
      *The Nature and Function of Tasks 3 in a Seminary*
      *Text-Community.* . . . . . . . . . . . . . . . . . . . . . . . . . . . . . . . . . . . . . . . . . . 45

2. THE SEMINARY AS A TEXTUAL COMMUNITY: REFLECTIONS ON
   JOHN SAILHAMER'S VISION FOR THEOLOGICAL EDUCATION . . . . . . . . . . .47
   Setting: Envisioning the Task of Theological Education . . . . . . . . . . . . . . 47
   Substance: Crafting the Coherence of a Seminary Curriculum . . . . . . . 50
   Significance: Reflecting on the Strategic Value of this Vision for
   Theological Education . . . . . . . . . . . . . . . . . . . . . . . . . . . . . . . . . . . . . . . . . 52

    *Defining the Seminary as a Textual Community* .................. 52
    *The Strategic Significance of Biblical Hermeneutics* ............... 56
    *Further Implications of the Vision for Seminary Curricula* ......... 60
    Shared Concerns: Dialogue Partners in an Ongoing Conversation .... 63
        *The Textual Community and the Culture of Theology*.............. 64
        *The World of the Text and the Drama of Doctrine* ................. 66
        *Biblical Theology and the Shape of a Curriculum* ................. 67
        *Theological Training and the Life of the Churches*................. 69
    Closing Reflection .................................................71

3. HERMENEUTICS, HISTORY, AND DISCIPLINARY DIALOGUE IN
   SAILHAMER'S SCHOLARSHIP ........................................75

4. WHAT HAVE THEY DONE TO MY GENESIS? ...........................83
   Old Story, New Perspective ........................................ 84
   The Lens of Faith .................................................. 85

5. READING THE BIBLE AS A TEXT......................................87

6. ARCHAEOLOGY AND THE RELIABILITY OF THE OLD TESTAMENT........93

7. COSMIC MAPS, PROPHECY CHARTS, AND THE HOLLYWOOD MOVIE:
   A BIBLICAL REALIST LOOKS AT THE ECLIPSE OF OLD TESTAMENT
   NARRATIVE...................................................... 101
   1. Introduction...................................................101
   2. The Biblical Story.............................................. 102
       *2.1. "Cosmic Maps"* ............................................ 102
       *2.2. How Are "Cosmic Maps" Formed? Three Examples from My Own
       Personal Experience* ......................................... 106

8. JOHANN AUGUST ERNESTI: THE ROLE OF HISTORY IN BIBLICAL
   INTERPRETATION ................................................ 121
   Introduction.....................................................121
   History of Interpretation .........................................122
       *1. Introduction*................................................122
       *2. A Review of the History of the Use of the Terms "Grammatical"
       and "Historical"*............................................. 124
   Johann August Ernesti ...........................................132
   Conclusion...................................................... 138

9. ENGAGING THE DISCIPLINES: SELECTED BOOK REVIEWS ............. 141
   Review of Gordon Wenham, *Genesis 1–15* (*Word Biblical
   Commentary; Word Books, 1987*). .................................141
   Review of Gordon Wenham, *Story as Torah: Reading the Old
   Testament Ethically* (*T&T Clark, 2000*)......................... 149

*Review of Joachim Schaper*, Eschatology in the Greek Psalter
(*Mohr Siebeck, 1995*).................................................. 152

*Review of Richard S. Hess and M. Daniel Carroll, eds.*, Israel's
Messiah in the Bible and the Dead Sea Scrolls (*Baker, 2003*) ......157

*Review of Hans-Joachim Kraus*, Systematische Theologie im
Kontext biblischer Geschichte und Eschatologie (*Neukirchener
Verlag, 1983*) ...................................................... 161

10. FINDING MEANING IN THE PENTATEUCH: AN INTERVIEW WITH
    COLLIN HANSEN .................................................. 167

11. THE WRITINGS OF JOHN H. SAILHAMER: A COMPREHENSIVE
    BIBLIOGRAPHY ................................................... 173
    Dissertation ..................................................... 173
    Books ............................................................ 173
    Articles and Essays .............................................. 174
    Book Reviews ..................................................... 176
    Papers and Presentations ......................................... 177
    Interviews ....................................................... 177

AFTERWORD: *Steven A. McKinion* ....................................... 179

ACKNOWLEDGMENTS ....................................................... 183

SCRIPTURE INDEX ....................................................... 187

PERSON INDEX .......................................................... 189

# Preface

In the fall of 1999, I (Jason) began teaching at Southeastern Baptist Theological Seminary. As a new faculty member at a large seminary, I was excited about teaching the students who were preparing for pastoral ministry. Coming back to the States from my PhD studies in Scotland, I was also looking forward to learning the craft of teaching from my faculty colleagues. As providence would have it, one of those new colleagues, John Sailhamer, had just joined the faculty that year also. One of my techniques for picking up teaching and research tips from my senior colleagues was to bring my books to the faculty lounge and hang out near the coffee machine. I could usually get in one or two questions before they had rinsed their mugs and poured the next cup.

One day, John poured a cup and then actually sat down in the lounge across from me. He asked me about my research interests. I said something about historical theology, particularly the history of interpretation. Hearing my reply, John asked me a question. "So, Jason, do you interpret the Bible like any other book?" Without taking the time to reflect on the question, I enthusiastically respond, "Yes!" I thought I understood the place of general hermeneutics. John grinned and said, "Hmm, I would have thought that you affirmed the Bible as inspired." Sailhamer's playful exchange would be a life-changing moment for me.

As I had done for other senior colleagues, I began reading Sailhamer's work so that I could have more meaningful exchanges with him. That reading plan lead me to a deeper dive into a confessional approach to hermeneutics and into the composition of biblical texts. My reading allowed me to pepper John with questions almost on a daily basis for the next couple of years. He graciously entertained my questions and even allowed me to push back on various ideas that he had.

Not all of my conversations with John were about hermeneutics and composition. Sometimes he told some interesting personal stories from his past. Some of his favorites were stories about being the son of a minister, his early job working for the Dallas Morning News, and how when he was in high school he did not know who the Beatles were (kind of a real-life version of the film Yesterday). One day he treated my colleague, Steve McKinion, and me to a story of how he was once offered the job as provost at Dallas Theological Seminary, and how he ultimately decided not to take the job. Steve and I would later kid him about his "Provost for a Day" experience in our frequent dialogue sessions with him. As always, John took the good-natured ribbing in stride.

In addition to the conversations that John and I had on biblical theology, the composition of biblical texts, and the value of textual features in interpretation, we also talked about the need for churches and seminaries to have more of a "text-based" model of discipleship or training in Bible reading. Eventually, I left the seminary faculty to join a pastoral staff in another state where we were going to attempt to see this text-oriented discipleship come to fruition in a local church. After a few, good years in that venture, I returned to teaching in higher education where I have spent the past fifteen years teaching hermeneutics and the value of a textual theology. In my most recent teaching post, our faculty has attempted to develop a M.Div. curriculum around a text-centered approach. Again, Sailhamer had a hand in shaping that vision, but I will leave that story for Ched to explain.

Fifteen years ago, I (Ched) took a course on biblical hermeneutics with Jason that included *Introduction to Old Testament Theology: A Canonical Approach*. During our class readings and discussions, I was struck by the insightful way that Sailhamer and this course reoriented us to the significance of the inspired Scriptures and the strategic importance of hermeneutics for biblical studies and ministry in the churches. After this course, I began to read more of Sailhamer's works and started to compile a comprehensive bibliography of his writings. I was able to compile a working bibliography of his published books, essays, articles, and reviews. At some point, though, I came across a syllabus online from one of his old courses that included some helpful comments about Jesus as the Messiah. What other resources like this might be available somewhere?

In searching through the library databases of places Sailhamer had studied or taught, I tried the catalog of the library at Dallas Theological Seminary in Dallas, TX. After sifting through the published material, I saw a listing for a manuscript titled, "The Nature, Purpose, and Tasks of a Theological Seminary." I had never seen this title before and immediately knew I needed to chase this down. Because it was Taco Tuesday and there was a Rosa's Cafe that I frequented when I visited DTS, this was an easy decision to make the trip from Fort Worth to Dallas. Sure enough, there at the end of a row on the long-term storage stacks in the Turpin Library was a folder with a full, 46 page address from 1993 by Sailhamer that appeared to have been composed on an old-school type-writer and photocopied for the bound library volume.

Both the taco plate and this unpublished address turned out to be a feast! Here was a vision for theological education that sought to allow a relentless focus on the text of Scripture to shape the pedagogy and curriculum of the entire program of study for those training for both the churches and the academy. For many years, I've thought about this address, discussed it with colleagues, and returned to it as I have been involved in theological education as a student and as a professor. Because of its significance as an unpublished work of Sailhamer and also as a substantial and insightful work on its own terms, I've long thought that others might want to consider this vision for theological education and seek to put into practice what is envisioned here. Our hope is that by publishing this address, you might benefit from this sustained argument that our approach to the Scriptures can also shape our approach to academic ministry within the context of seminaries and the churches.

The first part of the present volume includes the full text of Sailhamer's unpublished address and also a follow-up essay that reflects on the setting, substance, and significance of this new work. In part two, we include some of Sailhamer's lesser known works that focus on the use of history and hermeneutics with an eye toward the nature of biblical narratives. This section also includes some of Sailhamer's interaction with works from several different disciplines (from biblical studies to systematic theology) as well as his reflections on the state of Old Testament studies. These sections illustrate and inform some of the central contentions Sailhamer makes in his vision for theological education. The volume ends with the comprehensive bibliography of Sailhamer's writings that led to the discovery of this unpublished work these years ago.

As the editors, we are grateful to kindness of the Sailhamer family in letting us publish this address. We appreciate his wife Patty along with his children David, Elizabeth (Betsy), Peter, and John for sharing Dr. Sailhamer (again) with his former colleagues and students.

*Ched Spellman and Jason K. Lee*
*Cedarville, OH, January 2021*

# Foreword

*Stephen G. Dempster*

My first encounter with John Sailhamer was in reading his book *Introduction to Old Testament Theology: A Canonical Approach*.[1] I had just finished a sabbatical in which I had written a series of articles on the extraordinary fact of the Old Testament Canon. I had immersed myself in the Hebrew Bible and I was amazed at what I saw.

Trained as an exegete to see texts rather atomistically—as the individual trees in the forest so to speak, I had not appreciated their larger context—the sweep of the forest, and with this new vantage point, the independent and isolated pieces were now viewed as part of a larger whole. I came to understand that the New Testament writers were not proof-texting but were explicating a Text, in which individual texts were not autonomous fragments but formed part of a grander and intricate pattern.

When I read John's work, I was excited and saw that he had already seen some of the same things. A few years later I met him in person at a conference. He listened to a paper I gave and greatly encouraged me to turn it into a book, which was about seeing the hermeneutical forest and not just the exegetical trees.[2] I was amazed at not only his breadth of knowledge but his profound humility. Over the course of a number of years, I would send him articles and he would give me helpful and encouraging feedback. He became an effective dialogue partner for understanding the Old Testament.

---

[1] John H. Sailhamer, *Introduction to Old Testament Theology: A Canonical Approach* (Zondervan, 1995).

[2] Stephen G. Dempster, *Dominion and Dynasty: A Biblical Theology of the Hebrew Bible*, New Studies in Biblical Theology 15 (InterVarsity Press, 2003).

When I think of John, I automatically think of the Hebrew Bible, his complete mastery over its details and his ability to see beyond those particulars to its final shape and its significance. Of course, he saw the little details such as the Septuagint's witness to the Messiah in Numbers 24 where the Greek reads Gog instead of MT's Agag.[3] Or the use of a different verbal form to make a point in Genesis 15, that the narrator is supplying commentary.[4] But John never stopped there. He saw all of these details in the light of the larger canonical shape which had a beginning, middle, and end, and was not just a patchwork of individual sources drawn from diverse places and times, a sort of literary potpourri, but a book, the product of an Intelligent Design(er).

He was concerned not about *strata* but about *strategy*. Thus these individual texts assumed major significance in the larger storyline. The first word at the beginning of the first book of the Bible (רֵאשִׁית) is echoed at the end of the first book in Jacob's deathbed blessing to his children looking to the future of an Israelite king who will bless the world (אַחֲרִית).[5] Beginning leads to the end, the last days of history. Therefore, the Fall is not a dead end for the canon—not a *tragedy* but the beginning of a *trajectory* from the beginning to the end of history. Similarly, the first act of violence in Scripture is divine violence committed against animal life whose carcasses produce permanent clothing to cover the shame and sin of our first parents. Instead of their death, animals are slain in their place, the first step which will end in God's own death to clothe human beings with his own righteousness.[6]

But John was also heavily invested in the New Testament, where the trajectory begun in the Old Testament reaches its completion. His

---

3 Num 24:7. See John H. Sailhamer, *The Pentateuch as Narrative* (Zondervan, 1995), 229.

4 In Gen. 15:6, instead of the expected *wayyiqtol* form for Abraham's faith, there is a *weqatal* form. See Sailhamer, *Pentateuch as Narrative*, 151–52.

5 Gen 1:1, 49:1. See John Sailhamer, "Creation, Genesis 1-11, and the Canon," *Bulletin for Biblical Research* 10 (2000): 89–106.

6 John Sailhamer, "The Messiah and the Hebrew Bible," *Journal of the Evangelical Theological Society* 44 (2001): 9. John cites Johan Christian von Hoffman, "It is a long way between the death of an animal whose skin covered [man's] nakedness, and the death of the Son of God whose righteousness covers [man's] sin. Yet these are like the beginning and the end of the same journey."

email address was tnkntx@gmail.com, which I took for Tanak plus New Testament as one text. In his writings he tried to show that it is one matter to read the Old Testament in the light of the New Testament as is the habit of many Christians (i.e. if they read the Old Testament at all!) and quite another matter to read the New Testament in the light of the Old. The New Testament was not so much a guide to understand the Old Testament as the goal for understanding the Old Testament.[7] In other words, if we do not understand the Old Testament's depiction of the Messiah, we will not recognize the New Testament picture of Jesus.[8]

And this is exactly what the Master Exegete himself said when he rebuked his dull disciples on the Emmaus Road for not comprehending the significance of the recent events in Jerusalem—the death and reported resurrection of their rabbi, Jesus of Nazareth. With anyone with eyes to see, this death and resurrection, said their strange Visitor, were the exclamation point on and climax to the central theme of Israel's Bible. And it was nothing less than this "exegesis" which removed the veil from their eyes so that they were now able to understand their Bible.[9]

Three other words that come to mind when I think of John are words which he used for a chapter in one of his books: "Context is Everything."[10] In particular, by context he does not just mean how the literary placement of a text influences how it is understood, but that Scripture itself presents to us a context for understanding historical events. John saw so perceptively how the biblical understanding has been swallowed up by history so much so that evangelicals have fit the great story of God found in Scripture into a largely western narrative of pursuing the American dream.[11] He saw perceptively how the

---

7 John H. Sailhamer, *The Meaning of the Pentateuch: Revelation, Composition and Interpretation* (InterVarsity Press, 2009), 233.

8 Ibid.

9 Luke 24:13-49.

10 See John Sailhamer, *Genesis Unbound: A Provocative New Look at the Creation Account* (Multnomah Books, 1996). "Context is Everything" is the title of chapter seven.

11 What would he have thought of Donald Trump holding up a Bible in front of a historic church in Washington last summer?! See his essay from the *Criswell Theological Journal* in this volume: "Cosmic Maps, Prophecy Charts, and the Hollywood Movie."

enlightenment view of history had swallowed up the Bible's salvation history, and this had become the default position of both liberal and evangelical scholarship.

Accordingly, in evangelical circles the Bible is not read anymore as the ultimate context but is simply used as a means for apologetics, or devotions to help one get on with the business of living successfully in a world defined by the culture. In this respect I have come to see that John did not want to derogate the importance of history but wished to see history through the lens of the Text.

Consequently, there are many historical explanations of the Egyptian plagues, but what does the Text say? We may not know the name of the Pharaoh of the Exodus but what matters to the Text? That was a relatively unimportant fact for the Text. Instead, the Text chooses to elevate marginal people in the culture to the foreground. The Hebrew midwives are named! What does this mean? Moreover, to read the Torah with a focus on the major event of Sinai without seeing it in the context of the Text's final shape is somehow to fail to understand it. With its comprehensive description of 613 laws (the trees), it is easy to lose sight of their larger context (the forest), which witnesses to the failure of the Sinai covenant and the necessity of a new covenant in which the heart is circumcised to do the will of Yahweh. Indeed, context *is* everything.

John's emphasis on knowing the original languages of Scripture and its logical concomitant, the importance of the Text, is crucial for the future of theological education as recent works have shown the bifurcation of theology from exegesis of the Bible. They are viewed as two separate worlds as the academy has become separated from the church. For John, theology must be informed by exegesis and in particular biblical theology. His work on the final shape of the canon is a masterful work on biblical theology which is informed by the structure of the canon. Its final editors produced a theological document oriented to the coming of the Messiah. But this conclusion was driven ultimately by John's view of the canon: it was not and is not a collection of antiquated historical data from an ancient society. It is a living Word of revelation which speaks through the centuries—one can see this most clearly in the interpretive traditions, and also even in the history of the Text—and addresses us today.

The church needs to be vitally connected to this Text if it wants to be faithful to its mission. This is the pressing need for the church. This will result in prophetic preaching, teaching, and instruction which will enable believers to see their present moment in the light of the Eternal. John had come to see this probably not so much because he had mastered the Text, but because in the end, the Text had mastered him.

# Part One:
# Hermeneutics and Theological Education

# 1

# The Nature, Purpose, and Tasks of a Theological Seminary

*John H. Sailhamer*

THE FOLLOWING PAPER IS A DISCUSSION of the nature, purpose, and tasks of a theological seminary.[1] The approach it envisions is conservative, in that it values past efforts to construct a comprehensive seminary curriculum, though it is anything but an attempt to preserve the status quo. Along with many others who are currently rethinking the nature and purpose of a seminary education, we agree that in large measure present seminary programs at best often lack a cohesive center and are otherwise often incoherent or, in some cases, irrational.[2]

The underlying purpose of this paper is to provide a theoretical and reflective basis for designing a coherent and cohesive seminary curriculum (both explicit and implicit). As such the paper is, at places, admittedly abstract. The point of these abstract discussions, however, is always and only to ground our thinking about seminary education in biblical and social realities. The fact that our actions and programs,

---

1 *Ed:* In the text of this address, no wording has been revised. The editorial changes mostly relate to fuller references for abbreviated works, the introduction of a small number of paragraph breaks and section headings, the combining of footnotes for clarity, and a standardized citation style. The numbering of the headings has also been simplified and standardized. For instance, the heading "2.1.2.3.2.4.2.3" simply becomes a sub-heading that is positioned within the originally designed structure. Any changes that are outside of these parameters are explicitly marked in the footnotes (usually in italics and preceded by "*Ed:*"). On translations: any translation given of a non-English text in the main body of the essay or in the footnotes is Sailhamer's translation.

2 Markus Braun, following Gerhard Ebeling, has argued that the current shape of theological education is the result of the fragmentation of theology into a series of isolated disciplines. See Markus Braun, *Reformation des Theologie Studiums* (Herbert Reich Evangelischer Verlag, 1966). More recently a similar assessment has been advanced by Edward Farley, *Theologia: Fragmentation and Unity of Theological Education* (Fortress Press, 1983).

if rational, are linked to abstract principles and revealed truth, makes this aspect of curriculum design mandatory for a theological seminary, especially an evangelical one. The purpose of a theological seminary is directly linked to its nature as a part of the Christian Church and that, in turn, is related to certain fundamental principles. Thus, we will begin with a broad discussion of the seminary within the context of the church and the Word of God.

This paper will also argue that the nature and task of a Christian seminary is fundamentally hermeneutical—teaching the written Word of God. However, the approach taken in this paper will attempt to develop further the nature of that task by applying insights gained from contemporary analysis of social structures (particularly the role that authoritative texts play in the formation of text-communities) and hermeneutical theory (phenomenology of texts and text theory).[3] By viewing the written Word of God as a component in a larger whole of the the seminary text-community, it is argued that all departments which participate in the seminary curriculum share the same theoretical task (interpretation of texts) and differ only with respect to the aspect of the social structure (text-community) where it is applied. Thus, the actual responsibilities of *every* department are fundamentally practical.

We will proceed in two stages. First, we will discuss the nature and purpose of a theological seminary within the context of the church. Second, building on these earlier conclusions, we will discuss specific aspects of seminary education as they relate to the seminary's task in the future.

## Part One: The Nature and Purpose of a Seminary Text-Community

### 1. The Seminary and the Christian Church

Though it has links to numerous other institutions (e.g., Academia), the seminary, as such, exists *because of* and *in behalf of* the Christian church.

---

3 Two works on text theory have formed the basis of the analysis presented here: Siegfried J. Schmidt, *Texttheorie: Probleme einer Linguistik der sprachlichen Kommunikation*, Second Edition (Wilhelm Fink Verlag, 1976); and Robert de Beaugrande and Wolfrang Dressler, *Introduction to Text Linguistics* (Longman, 1981).

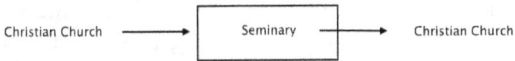

Thus, the nature of Christianity necessarily defines the nature and purpose of a Christian seminary. This was true long before the seminary consciously began to define itself in terms of that relationship.[4] The essential links between the seminary and the Christian church mandate that we understand the nature and purpose of a seminary from within the larger question of, What is Christianity? What is its essential nature (*Wesen*) as a religion?[5]

There are many ways to address this question. It can, for example, be approached theologically, as in classical orthodoxy,[6] historically (e.g., Harnack), sociologically (Durkheim, Berger),[7] and phenomenologically (Widengren, Gadamer, Ricoeur).[8] Fortunately for our purposes

---

4 See Friedrich Schleiermacher, *Brief Outline of the Study of Theology*, trans. William Farrer (T&T Clark, 1850). Theological schools, as such, can be traced at least as far back as the early Klosterschulen and the Rule of St. Augustine (apx. 6th cent.). Already in the Rule of Pachomius (apx. 290–346), theological formation (Bildung) was mandated: (#80) *Omino nullus erit in monasterio, qui non discat literas et de scripturis aliquid teneat*.

5 A large and impressive literature has grown up around this question ranging from Johann Arndt's, *True Christianity* (1610; trans: Paulist Press, 1979) to Adolf Harnack's, *What is Christianity? (Wesen des Christentums)* (1900; trans: Harper & Row, 1957). In viewing Christianity as a "religion" we are not suggesting it is *only* a religion. We are only recognizing that it is at least a "religion" in the technical sense of the term.

6 Classical theology distinguishes the essence of Christianity *materially*, Catholics being satisfied with a straightforward identification of Christianity with the visible Church hierarchy while Protestants speak of various forms of the kingdom of God, that is, ranging from the idea of a personal relationship with God through faith in Christ (*solus Christus, sola gratia*) to, with Albrecht Ritschl, a realization of God's kingdom in the political institutions of the modern world; or *formally*, the written Scriptures (*sola scriptura*). Lutherans tend toward a material and Reformed toward a formal understanding of Christianity, though both acknowledge the logical priority of the formal principle. See Christoph Ernst Luthardt, *Kompendium der Dogmatik* (Dörffling & Franke, 1900), 18–26.

7 Emile Durkheim, *The Elementary Forms of the Religious Life* (Collier Macmillan Publishers, 1965); Peter L. Berger, *The Social Reality of Religion* (Faber and Faber, 1967).

8 Hans-Georg Gadamer, *Wahrheit und Methode* (Mohr-Siebeck, 1975); Paul Ricoeur, *The Conflict of Interpretations: Essays in Hermeneutics*, ed. Don Idhe

all of these major approaches agree on what is the fundamental characteristic of Christianity.[9] Christianity, like Judaism and Islam, is a *Schriftreligion*, a religion of the Book.[10] This was clearly spelled out by the early theologians and is accepted as the essence of Christianity in modern theology.[11] Karl Barth, for example, in agreement with classical orthodoxy, aptly argued this point in opposition to theological liberalism, "If in reply it is asked whether Christianity is really a book-religion, the answer is that strangely enough Christianity has always been and only been a living religion when it is not ashamed to be actually and seriously a book-religion."[12] Calvin argued the same

---

(Northwestern University Press, 1974); and Geo Widengren, *Religionsphänomenologie* (Walter de Gruyter & Co., 1969), 1: "Die Religionsphänomenologie will die verschieden Erscheinungen der Religion klassifiziern, d.h. sie will die Religion so schildern, wie sie in ihren wechselnden Lebensäusserungen erscheint. . . . Die Religionsphänomenologie Bemüht sich, eine zusammenfassende Darstellung aller wechselnden Erscheinungen der Religion zu geben und wird hierdurch zur systamatischen Ergänzung der Religionsgeschichte."

9 I am referring here specifically to a fundamental characteristic rather than a distinctive or defining characteristic because in terms discussed here, Christianity shares the same basic characteristic with both Judaism and Islam, that is, they are fundamentally defined in terms of their relationship to an authoritative text.

10 Widengren, *Religionsphänomenologie*, 569.

11 Calvin: "*Hoc igitur singular donum est, ubi ad erudiendam ecclesiam non mutis duntaxat magistris Deus utitur, se dos quoque sacrosanctum reserat. . . . Hunc ordinem ab initio erga ecclesiam suam tenuit ut praeter communia illa documenta, verbum quoque adhiberet, quae rectior est et certior ad ipsum dignoscendum nota*" (*Institutio Christianae Reglüonis*, I, VI, 1); Johan Friedrich König (1664): "Religio christiana est ratio colendi deum verum fide in christum et caritate erga deum et proximum, secundum verbum scriptum, ut homo a deo avulsus deo reduniatur" (Carl Heinz Ratschow, *Lutherische Dogmatik zwischen Reformation und Aufklärung*, Teil I [Gütersloher Verlagshaus Gerd Mohn, 1964], 58).

12 Karl Barth, *Church Dogmatics*, Vol. 1, Part 2 (T&T Clark, 1956), 494–495. No less a classical liberal than Adolph Harnack, however, acknowledged the textual nature of the Christian religion in Protestantism: "Protestantism was a *Reformation*, that is to say, a renewal, as regards the core of the matter, as regards religion. . . . Religion was . . . *reduced* to its essential factors, to the Word of God and to faith. . . . The community assembled for God's worship must not solemnize its worship in any other way than by proclaiming the Word and by prayer. To this, however, we must add, according to the Reformers' injunctions, that all that is to stamp this community as a Church is its existence as a community of the faith in which God's Word is preached aright . . . community is based upon the Gospel alone, but that the Gospel is contained in Holy Scripture" (Harnack, *What is Christianity*, 269–274).

point in commenting on 2 Corinthians 5:7, "For we *see*, indeed, but it is *through a glass darkly* (1 Cor 13:12) that is, in place of the reality itself we rest upon the Word."[13]

One further comment: the central importance of the textual nature of Christian religion does not replace or diminish the centrality of Christ (*solus Christus*) or the Gospel (*sola gratia*) to Christianity. On the contrary, what we are suggesting is that these central elements of the Christian religion are themselves textual in nature.[14] The importance of the written Word to Christian self-identity, in fact, includes, but goes far beyond, the Reformers' call to return to the original sources or the question of the role of tradition in the life of the Church. Thus, quite apart from the Protestant principle of *sola scriptura*, the textual nature of Christianity's *theologia*, whether Catholic or otherwise, is beyond dispute, especially in Evangelicalism.[15]

---

13 Latin: *"videmus enim, sed in speculo et aenigmate; hoc est loco rei in verbo acquiescimus"* (quoted by Barth, *Church Dogmatics*, Vol. 1, Part 2, 494–495).

14 Paul Ricoeur, from the viewpoint of continental philosophy and hermeneutics, has forcefully argued the case for a textual understanding as the essence of Christianity: "There has always been a hermeneutic problem in Christianity because Christianity proceeds from a proclamation ... this fundamental preaching, this word, comes to us through writings, through the Scriptures, and these must constantly be restored as the living word if the primitive word that witnessed to the fundamental and founding event is to remain contemporary.... This relation between writing and the word and between the word and the event and its meaning is the crux of the hermeneutics problem. But this relation itself appears only through a series of interpretations. These interpretations constitute the history of the hermeneutic problem and even the history of Christianity itself, to the degree that Christianity is dependent upon its successive readings of Scripture and on its capacity to reconvert this Scripture into the living word" (*Conflict of Interpretation*, 382).

15 I am using the term *theologia* in the sense given it by Farley, *Theologia*, but stated more directly by Gerhard Ebeling, *Wort und Glaube*, 2nd Edition (Mohr-Siebeck, 1962), 480: "Theology is an indivisible whole because it has to do with a fundamental simplicity: the Word of God, which is not multivarious but a simple unity. A division of theology into distinct disciplines is meaningful only when each discipline is understood, not as a part of the whole, but as a realization of the whole" ("Die Theologie ist ein unteilbares Ganzes, weil sie es mit einem Einzigen, Grundeinfachen zu tun hat: dem Worte Gottes, das nicht vielerlei, sondern eines ist. Eine Gliederung der Theologie in verschiedene Aufgabenbereiche ist ... sinnvoll, wenn jede Teilaufgabe verstehbar ist als seine solche, in der das Ganze latent ist"). For a discussion of the importance of the textual nature of Christianity's *theologia* to evangelicalism, see the

## Excursus: Edward Farley's *Theologia*

In my opinion, a central weakness of Edward Farley's essay on *theologia* is his failure to adequately note the textuality of Christianity's *theologia*. In large measure this was owing to his notion that in premodern conceptualizations of *theologia* there were *two* fundamentally different senses of the term "theology," that is, *theologia* understood as knowledge and *theologia* understood as a discipline.[16] In making such a distinction, Farley inevitably, and perhaps inadvertently, severed at least a part of Christianity's *theologia* from its roots in scriptural revelation.[17] He thus, inaccurately in my opinion, understands *theologia*, qua knowledge as "an actual, individual cognition of God and things related to God, a cognition which in most treatments attends faith and has eternal happiness as its final goal."[18] It is in this sense that Farley understands theology as a *habitus*, that is, "a cognitive disposition and orientation of the soul, a knowledge of God and what God reveals. . . . A practical, not theoretical, habit having the primary character of wisdom."[19]

A glance at the standard theological works of the period is enough, however, to call Farley's thesis into serious question.[20] In the Reformed

---

introduction to my book, *The Pentateuch as Narrative: A Biblical and Theological Commentary* (Zondervan, 1992), 16–22.

16  Farley, *Theologia*, 31.

17  Farley is somewhat inconsistent in suggesting this because he concedes elsewhere that theology qua knowledge "is connected with insight into Scripture and that in turn is served by commentaries on Scripture" (*Theologia*, 36). It is "a wisdom which can be prompted, deepened, and extended by human study and argument" (37).

18  Farley, *Theologia*, 31. Farley, mistakenly I believe, confuses the scholastic notion of *theologia visionis* (*theologia beatorum*), that knowledge of God which Christians (will) have in the eternal state, and *theologia revelationis* (*theologia viatorum*) or, that knowledge of God which Christians have in this life (cf. Francis Turretin, *Institutio Theologiae Elenticae* [John D. Lowe, 1685], 6).

19  Farley, *Theologia*, 35. The influence of the personalism of classical liberalism and the existentialism of modern theology can be seen in Farley's summary of the Christian *theologia* of the second period: "The most important point is that in the second period theology characteristically refers to a practical, salvation-oriented (existential-personal) knowledge of God" (*Theologia*, 36).

20  Farley himself acknowledges that the distinction he is attempting to make is not noted in the reference literature, a fact which should, in itself, raise the question of its validity (see *Theologia*, 45n4).

theology represented by Turrettin's *Elencticae*, for example, *theologia* is divided into that knowledge of God which is noted *systematice* (a body of wholesome teaching about God and divine things drawn from Scripture) and that which is noted *habitualiter* ("... by means of a capacity resident in the human mind").[21] Though on the surface these categories seem to parallel Farley's own description, there is, in fact, no indication that the latter (capacity of the human mind; *habitus in intellectu*) is fundamentally of a different kind than the former (a body of wholesome teaching; *compages doctrinae*) or that the latter (capacity of the human mind; *habitus in intellectu*) is not related to reflection on Scripture and commentary. On the contrary, Turrettin, in fact, viewed the *habitus theologiae* only as a means (*per modum*) of knowing *theologia*, not as a form of knowledge itself.[22] On the Lutheran side, König distinguished between *theologia* understood both "absolutely, in so far as it is a capacity of the soul" and accidentally, in so far as it is a body of teaching or an area of study.[23] Thus *theologia* is understood both as a thing (*res*) and as a process of the formation of doctrine.[24]

## Summary

To summarize from what has been said thus far, the Christian *theologia*, with which the seminary has been and is entrusted, is fundamentally *textual* in nature and as such it exists by means of reflection on Holy Scripture and commentary. This, it seems to me, has far reaching implications for the nature, purpose, and task of a theological seminary.

---

21 Latin: "... *compagem doctrinae salutaris de Deo et rebus divinis ex Scriptura expressae ... per modum habitus in intellectu residentis*" (*Institutio Theologiae Elencticae*, 6).

22 See *Institutio Theologiae Elencticae*, 6 (Locus I, Quest. II).

23 See Johann Friedrich König, *Theologia Positiva Acroamatica* (1664), quoted in Ratschow, *Lutherische Dogmatik*, Part I, 28: "*absolute, qua est habitus anmi ... accidentaliter, qua doctrine vel disciplina es*" (§27).

24 See Ratschow, *Lutherische Dogmatik*, 31: "Diese theologia, absolute angesehen, ist ein habitus animi. Sie gehört also in den Bereich der intellektuellen Fähigkeiten des Menschen, das heißt, Theologie ist ein Denkvollzug."

## 2. The Seminary and the Scriptures

If the seminary, as such, exists because of and in behalf of the Christian Church, and if Christianity is a religion of the Book, then the seminary exists because of and in behalf of the Scriptures.

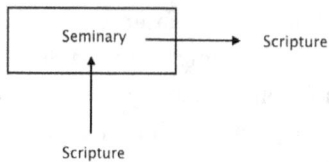

A seminary is, in this sense, a "textual community."[25] It exists within the context of what Thomas Mann once called the "quoted life" (*Zitathaftes Leben*), that is, a life that conceptualizes its own existence in terms of authoritative texts. Moreover, the role of the Scriptures as texts in the seminary community is more than a means of conceptualizing its Christian identity, it is, as well, constitutive of the seminary community itself. This is the sociological side of the textual community.[26]

There is also a hermeneutical component to the notion that the seminary is a textual community and this is seen most clearly in Gadamer's concept of the "effective history" of authoritative texts.[27] Texts such as the Bible are not merely preserved by or constitutive of faith communities like seminaries, it is precisely within these communities that they give shape to their own meaning. Unlike texts in general, authoritative texts operate within communities not by conforming themselves to the autonomous semantic structures of the community but by creating and nourishing the community's own text-specific

---

25 A "textual community" is a "community united by, indeed constituted by, a foundational text—the Christian Scriptures" (Kevin Vanhoozer, "The Community of Interpreters: Approaching the Text," an unpublished paper discussed at the 1990 Trinity Divinity School faculty retreat).

26 See Berger, *Social Reality of Religion*.

27 The principle of effective history (Das Prinzip der Wirkungsgeschichte) in Gadamer refers to the fact that an authoritative text, such as the Bible, has an effect on its readers in such a way that it influences and shapes further readings of that text. See Hans-Georg Gadamer, *Truth and Method* (Seabury Press, 1975), 267.

categories of meaning. It is these same categories which define the community itself.

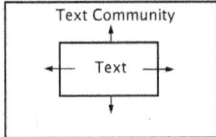

As we will see, this feature of a text-community greatly helps organize the assessment of the seminary both as a part of *academia* and *ecclesia*. For example, as we will see, the nature of the biblical text itself, as both human and divine, calls for a community that is both historical (academia) and theological (faith) at the same time.

Furthermore, there are a number of practical reasons why viewing the seminary from this perspective can be helpful in planning for its future. For one thing, it helps give concrete focus to the role of *theologia* in providing a sense of unity within the goals and objectives of a seminary curriculum. For example, in responding to the alleged dichotomy between the practical and theoretical departments a textually defined *theologia* means that at a fundamental level, every aspect of a seminary curriculum involves a similar task, that is, the interpretation (*traditio*) of Scripture (*traditum*).[28]

Surface tensions will inevitably continue to exist between departments in a seminary because there will always be wide divergences in specific contexts of application, but fundamentally, all departments within a seminary must fulfill the same task, the application of Scripture to life. Evangelism, the proclamation of the gospel, is first of all devoted to the interpretation of the Scriptures in which the Gospel is embodied. Homiletics clearly has the task of interpreting Scripture, but just as importantly, it also must construct a text, namely, the sermon, making it fundamentally textual on two counts. There is, then, a pervasive unity of purpose within a textual community such as a seminary in that each member is entrusted with the same theoretical problems—meaning in texts.

---

28 Cf. Michael Fishbane, *Biblical Interpretation in Ancient Israel* (Clarendon Press, 1985).

By the same token, in a seminary conceived of as a textual community, every aspect of the curriculum, e.g., Hebrew Exegesis, is also seen as practical, that is, an application of the text to a life situation. What is important to note is that the corollary concepts of "effective history" and "quoted life" discussed above, provide a genuine link to the application of scriptural texts to life settings. What exegesis is forced to face in a textual community is that the text and its meaning have, in actual fact, already played a major role in shaping the life setting to which it is being applied. That setting is the Christian church. This, it seems to me, is the lasting contribution of "canon criticism" to biblical and theological studies.[29]

The most arcane of all theological tasks is that of textual criticism, the study of textual variants in ancient manuscripts. Within a textual community, however, variant readings are seen as an index, nay a virtual taxonomy, of possible options for the application of Scripture to real-life situations. Though it has only recently been given the appreciation it deserves, it has long been recognized that the Hebrew Bible itself bears on every page the nicks and bruises of its constant use in living textual communities within both Judaism and Christianity.[30]

In virtually every messianic passage in the Hebrew Bible, for example, textual variants abound, reflecting not only the community's attempt to come to grips with its own identity (messianism and non-messianism within the Jewish community) but also the claims of other communities with respect to these same texts (e.g., Christians, Samaritans, Karaites, Muslims). Seen from this perspective, the dichotomy that often arises between exegesis of the Bible versus exegesis of culture, though problematic at one level, is thus resolved at another. In a text-community, exegesis of the Bible *is* an exegesis of culture.[31]

---

29 See James Sanders, "Adaptable for Life: The Nature and Function of Canon," in *Magnalia Dei: The Mighty Acts of God. Essays on Bible and Archaeology in Memory of G. E. Wright*, ed. Frank Moore Cross, et al (Doubleday, 1976), 531–560.

30 Cf. Abraham Geiger, *Urschrift und Übersetzungen der Bibel in ihrer Abhängigkeit von der inner Entwickelung des Judenthums* (Verlag von Julius Hainauer, 1857).

31 Cf. Geiger, *Urschrift und Übersetzungen*, 19: "In the same way as understanding of Jewish history contributes to our knowledge of the history of the Bible, a knowledge of the Bible's history cast light on the history of Judaism."

Moreover, at least in the western world, claims of a new paganism notwithstanding, exegesis of culture is an exegesis of the Bible.[32] The "secular city" is pervaded at every level by deep semantic structures drawn from the Bible.[33] These structures are not a mere biblical legacy from an earlier stage in culture; they are, in fact, continually being renewed and enlivened by social structures completely unrelated to active biblical communities such as Evangelicalism and Roman Catholicism and, by and large, they remain unimpeded by counter efforts of Liberal Christianity to de-emphasize the place of Scripture in modern culture.

A warning is perhaps in order: we are not speaking here of exegeting cultures rather than biblical texts, nor of exegeting cultures in order to understand the Bible. We are rather speaking of exegeting the Bible in order to understand the deep level semantic structures of those civilizations effected by the Bible, e.g., western civilization.[34]

In any case, viewing the seminary as a text community is important not because it makes disciplines such as Hebrew exegesis practical. On the contrary, it is only when, within a text community, exegesis is understood to be a practical hermeneutical task that it is even possible to think correctly about it. Exegesis of the Bible *is* exegesis of a text-in-context. The only real theoretical task that remains is that which is common to all disciplines, namely, the nature of interpretation itself (hermeneutics).

---

32 Cf. Northrop Frye, *The Great Code: The Bible and Literature* (Harcourt Brace Jovanovich, 1982), xii: "A student of English literature who does not know the Bible does not understand a good deal of what is going on in what he reads: the most conscientious student will be continually misconstruing the implications, even the meaning."

33 For example, see John Romer, *Testament: The Bible and History* (Konecky & Konecky, 1988).

34 I have in mind something along the lines of Henning Graf Reventlow's book, *The Authority of the Bible and the Rise of the Modern World* (Fortress Press, 1985), 413: "The history of philosophy also appears in a different light when we see more clearly than before the close connection between philosophical systems and contemporary theology. The significant role played by the interpretation of the Bible in the thinking of Hobbes, Spinoza or Locke, to mention only the best-known names, and indeed for scientists like Boyle and Newton, threatens to be forgotten too easily in today's world, for which the Bible seems so remote. To forget the role of the Bible in their thought makes it difficult to understand all these figures and even distorts their actual intention."

Viewing the seminary as a textual community can also assist in the task of projecting goals and ideals for the seminary into the future. Simply put, whatever the future may hold, the central task of the seminary always remains the same—the interpretation of Scripture. What will change is that which is already changing, the situation or cultural context in which ministry is carried out. If a seminary understands itself as a community created by and entrusted with an authoritative text, then it should stay its course for the future by means of that text, the Bible. This may mean the seminary will change "things" it is now doing in order to adjust for the future; but it means, more importantly, that the seminary should not change the basic "thing" it is doing as a text community, which is, "stick to the text." It is the text-in-situation nature of the seminary that will provide both the stability and force of the seminary's contribution to the church in the future, as well as the flexibility to meet whatever new situations arise.

It was, I believe, in this sense of the task of theological education that Karl Barth concluded his now famous last words to his students at Bonn. Having been removed from his teaching post in Bonn for refusing to sign a loyalty oath to Hitler, Barth delivered his farewell message to the students with these words: "And now the end has come. So listen to my last piece of advice: exegesis, exegesis and yet more exegesis! Keep to the Word, to the Scripture, which has been given us."[35] In giving this advice, Barth was surely not simply concerned that his students keep up with their exegetical skills in his absence. Quite apart from that, Barth clearly understood that the interpretation of Scripture was itself constitutive of the Christian Church and as such its survival as well as its impact on the dark events around them could only be effected through a "quoted life," that is, a life lived within the world defined and articulated by the text of Scripture.[36]

---

35 See Eberhard Busch, *Karl Barth's Lebenslauf* (Chr. Kaiser Verlag, 1975), 272: "Und nun ist das Ende gekommen.... Nehmen Sie jetzt.... meinen letzten Rat: Exegese, Exegese und noch einmal Exegese!... Halten Sie sich an das Wort, an die Schrift, die uns gegeben ist."

36 *Ed:* Regarding the "dark events," Sailhamer footnotes Barth's remark: "... aber siehe da: Es fiel ein Reif in der Frühlingsnacht!" (Busch, *Karl Barth's Lebenslauf,* 272).

I do not know how the seminaries of Europe responded to Karl Barth's plea, but, ironically, or providentially, it was just at this same time, 1935, that Dallas Theological Seminary was implementing its most fundamental and lasting curriculum change, the initiation of the four-year ThM degree.

## Summary

A seminary, as such, exists because of and in behalf of the Christian Church. If so, then a seminary exists because of and in behalf of our Lord and his Word. The purpose of a seminary is to glorify the Living Word of God who is known in the written Word of God. It does this specifically by preparing ministers of the Word.

It is important to emphasize that it is through the written Word that we come to know the Living Word. We know no other Christ Jesus than that One who is known in Scripture and we know no other Gospel than that which is in the Bible. There is thus a logical priority given to the Scriptures in defining the nature and purpose of the seminary. There may, of course, often be a temporal priority given to such aspects of the Christian life as prayer, worship, fellowship, and evangelism.

The seminary's curriculum is Scripture-based and its community life is Scripture-centered. All aspects of its purpose and goals are derived from Scripture. It is in this sense that the seminary is a "textual community." Thus, whatever the future may hold, the central task of the seminary always remains the same—the interpretation of Scripture.

### 3. THE SEMINARY AND THE ACADEMY

In this section we will discuss aspects of seminary which are implications of the description of a seminary given above. We will focus on the areas of Academia and Ecclesia. Our primary questions will be, What are the tasks which the seminary, as a text-community, should perform within Academia and Ecclesia? And, How does the concept of the seminary as a text-community affect the structure of the seminary?

## Academia et Ecclesia

In Academia, whose stronghold is the University, man is the measure of all things; in Ecclesia, God is Lord. There are other features that distinguish these two realms, but for our purposes it is enough to say that a defining characteristic of Academia is its horizontal set of allegiances whereas with Ecclesia, its allegiances are both vertical and horizontal.

In keeping with the nature of Scripture (both human and divine), the seminary, as a text-community, has a dual allegiance. In the first place, human beings wrote the Bible. Therefore, as a human product, the Bible has a legitimate place in the human sciences. It is widely recognized that the Bible, as an "objectification of life," has played a major role in the construction of the modern "historical world."[37] Second, as the product of divine inspiration (*theopneustia*), the Bible also has its place in Ecclesia. To state the matter in more abstract terms, Ecclesia recognizes that the Bible is not merely an objectification of life (as in Academia), it is, in fact, *the* objectification of life by which all others are measured.[38] It is, in other words, the canon of Scriptures which Ecclesia accepts as the Bible.

It is important in discussing both of these realms to bear in mind that for the seminary it is the Bible, *as the Word of God* (*theopneustia*) that finds its place in both Academia and Ecclesia. It must be stressed that this is quite a different sort of Bible than usually finds its way into Academia. Though the University may attempt to deal only with what it considers to be "the human side" of the Bible, and the religious community may feel it has need only of the "devotional," we maintain that such attempts are fundamentally flawed at the outset. The Bible cannot be divided in this way merely to allow it to exist in these two realms. The Bible is a unique book and as such requires a

---

37 See below for a discussion of this concept.

38 It is in this sense, I believe, that Auerbach argued that "the world of the Scripture stories is not satisfied with claiming to be historically true reality—it insists that it is the only real world.... Far from seeking, like Homer, merely to make us forget our own reality for a few hours, it seeks to overcome our reality: we are to fit our own life into its world, feel ourselves to be elements in its structure of universal history" (Erich Auerbach, *Mimesis: The Representation of Reality in Western Literature* [Princeton University Press, 1953], 15).

unique context.³⁹ We will contend in this section of the paper that it is precisely this feature of the Bible, being both human and divine, that makes the seminary text-community essential for both Academia and Ecclesia.

## The Function of the Seminary Text-Community within Academia

Under this heading our aim is to discuss the rationale, responsibility, and contribution of the seminary's participation in the realm of Academia, as well as the general nature and purpose of that contribution. We will begin with a review of the main lines of argument for viewing the seminary as Academia and then we will list some key tasks which this role presents. As will be apparent, we understand the whole of the discussion to be an implication of the nature of the seminary as a text-community.

## The Rationale for the Academia in the Seminary

We turn first to the seminary's rationale for entering into the realm of Academia. What right does the seminary have to engage in the tasks of the Academia? We are using the term *Academia* in its technical sense of the sciences, or, more specifically, "the human sciences." Traditionally this realm has been the primary focus and responsibility of the University. Since the first half of the 17$^{th}$ century, universities have increasingly adopted the methods of the natural sciences (e.g., mathematics, physics) in the definition and study of the human sciences and this has led to a great deal of uncertainty about the status of the human sciences within Academia. We do not intend to raise the general issue of the place of the human sciences within Academia, though we acknowledge that the question is essential to a proper understanding of the role of Academia in the seminary. We will be content here with a brief survey of the issue.

A crucial stage leading to the acceptance of the human sciences in the University was the recognition of a fundamental distinction between the natural sciences and the human sciences. It was argued,

---

39 This aspect of the Bible has been fully developed in the recently published work of Gerhard Maier, *Biblisch Hermeneutik* (R. Brockhaus Verlag, 1990).

moreover, that though the natural sciences and the human sciences were fundamentally different with respect to their objects, nature, and human beings respectively, they both, in their own way, had a legitimate right to the claim of being scientific. The claim of the human sciences, however, was not established by imitating the natural sciences. On the contrary, it came only from a proper appreciation of its object, the historical human being. The dilemma of the human sciences lay in the fact that both its subject (the scientist) and its object (human beings) were the same. This meant there was a "subjectivity of experience" which impeded a purely scientific (that is, detached) approach to the object. Such an object, the human being, if it were to be approached scientifically would have to be "objectified."

The concept of "objectification of life," originally proposed by Wilhelm Dilthey, has played a major role in legitimizing the human sciences (*Geisteswissenschaften*).[40] Put simply, Dilthey argued that although human beings as such cannot be the proper object of detached, scientific inquiry, it is possible to view objectively and externally, that which human beings have produced. Such objects of human activity can be viewed as the externalizations of human subjectivity (*Erlebnisse*): "Every word, every sentence, every gesture or polite formula, every work of art and every political deed is intelligible because the people who expressed themselves through them and those who understand them have something in common ... we ourselves are woven into this common sphere."[41]

Thus any human product becomes an object of the human sciences in and within the world of nature and is a proper object of scientific study. One can see that the net effect of this approach was to make the human sciences essentially hermeneutical. The "objectifications of life," whether they be texts, buildings, Freudian dreams, or survey questionnaires, must be interpreted.[42]

---

40 Wilhelm Dilthey, *Der Aufbau der Geschichtlichen Welt in den Geisteswissenschaften* (Suhrkamp Verlag, 1981), 177.

41 Dilthey, *Der Aufbau der Geschichtlichen Welt*, 178.

42 To quote Riceour, "It is the task of this hermeneutics to show that existence arrives at expression, at meaning, and at reflection only through the continual exegesis of all the significations that come to light in the world of culture. Existence becomes a self—human and adult—only by appropriating this meaning, which first

# The Nature, Purpose, and Tasks of a Theological Seminary

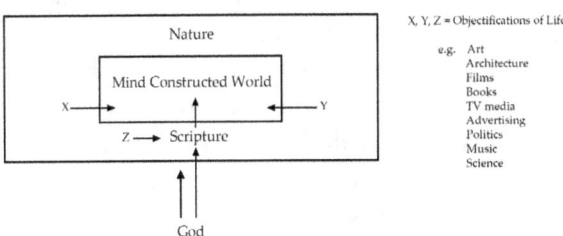

Given this criterion for participation in Academia, it is not hard to see that the study of the Bible can claim a valid place within it.[43] Who can dispute the fact that the Bible has played a decisive role in the shaping the "mind constructed world" which is the object of the human sciences? Moreover, by finding a place in Academia, the Bible also has earned the right as an object of inquiry in the University.

As far as I know, no one disputes this claim. What is disputed, however, is whether the seminary's Bible, *as the Word of God*, (*theopneustia*) has a place within Academia and the University. In the United States, at least, there is no place within the modern secular University for the Bible, *as the Word of God*. The causes for this are historical and legal, but hardly rational. The fact that the Bible in this sense is not welcome in the University, however, does not mean it has no place in Academia. We are here contending, as a matter of fact, that a proper study of the Bible as an object within the Academia can only be appreciated and carried out within the context of a text-community such as a theological seminary.

It should be clear from what we have suggested in the earlier part of this paper about the necessity of a sympathetic text-context for a proper exegesis of the Bible, that the University is not such a context. By its own admission it is not a community of faith, shaped by the Bible, nor is it willing to listen to *all* that the Bible has to say. The University, a text-community in its own right, will listen only to that part of the Bible which speaks of man and not to that part which speaks of

---

resides 'outside,' in works, institutions, and cultural moments in which the life of the spirit is objectified" (*Conflict of Interpretation*, 22).

43 We are including in the notion of the study of the Bible all the ancillary departments of the seminary, such as, Theology, Education, Homiletics, et al.

God.[44] Given its own self-identity, no one can dispute the University's right to approach the Bible in this way.

What must be stressed, however, is that, given the importance of understanding a text-in-context and the concept of "effective history," it is clear that from the start, the University is an unlikely place to seek a proper understanding of the Bible. By the same token, it should also be clear that the seminary is, in fact, an ideal context. As a part of the Christian church, the seminary is a text-community shaped by the Bible within a context of an effective history that lies unbroken from the time of its composition. For the social scientist, the church is to the Bible what a living informant is to an unknown language. The church is the living key to the Bible's meaning. It is in the nature of the seminary as a text-community, then, that we find a valid rationale for the seminary's commitment to Academia within its curriculum.

## The Responsibility of the Seminary to Academia

Does the seminary also have a responsibility to Academia within its curriculum? In answer to that question, we must be quick to admit that just because it is an ideal context for the academic study of the Bible, it does not necessarily follow that it is also the seminary's responsibility to do so. However, we maintain that the seminary does have a responsibility to Academia and that this responsibility to Academia stems directly from the message of the Bible itself. Though it could be developed at length, we will only mention the fact in broad outline.

A community which takes the Bible seriously cannot overlook the Bible's own preoccupation not only with God, but with mankind and nature. What this means is that, the object of the human sciences of Academia is of primary importance to the Bible. The idea of a biblical text-community turned in on itself (concerned only with Ecclesia) and away from the world (the object of Academia), would contradict the central message of Scripture. As a community constitutive of the Scriptures, it would, by definition, be an irrational community.

---

44 Cf. Ricoeur, *Conflict of Interpretation*, 387: "As soon as the whole Bible is treated like the *Iliad* or the Pre-Socratics, the latter is desacralized and the Bible is made to appear as the word of humans."

Because of this, we conclude that in the future the seminary should continue to focus its curriculum on the concerns of Academia. In a real sense, it would be irrational and unbiblical to do otherwise.

## The Contribution of the Seminary to Academia

From what has been said it should be clear that the seminary can make a major and unique contribution to Academia in its exegesis and exposition of the Bible, as well as its ancillary disciplines, e.g., Theology, Ethics, Church History, Education, and Homiletics. First, as a biblical text-community with an authentic effective history, the seminary provides an ideal setting for understanding the Bible and its contribution to the "mind constructed world" of Academia.

Second, the seminary text-community, as a community of faith, provides a valid and necessary "congeniality" for understanding the Bible as such.[45] The seminary need not claim exclusive rights to an appropriate congeniality with the biblical text, but it should insist on the recognition of the validity of the one it has.

Third, the seminary as a text-community *coram deo*, stands in submission to the text rather than as sovereign over the text as in the University. It is thus in a position to listen to and hear the text acutely.[46] It is in this regard that Stuhlmacher has called for an "openness to transcendence," by which he means "that we may not use the traditional historical method merely to inquire in critically one-sided fashion how *we* relate to the texts and how the texts . . . can be ranked in an

---

45  Cf. Walter Eichrodt, "Hat die alttestamentliche Theologie noch selbständige Bedeutung innerhalb der alttestamentlichen Wissenschaft?" *ZAW* (1929), 87: "It is clear that an inner relationship must exist between the investigator and his object in order to overcome its strangeness and to comprehend its essence (*Wesen*). By no means can one understand everything. One can understand only the sphere of human events with which one possesses an 'affinity.' Genuine understanding goes beyond empathy and imitation. . . . It comes only in the encounter between two similar lives. One is able to comprehend only that in which one participates in some way with one's likeness."

46  In classical hermeneutical theory, such as Rambach, it was prerequisite that, along with a thorough knowledge of the biblical languages, the interpreter be filled with a love for Jesus Christ (*amor Iesou Christi*) and a sincere love for God's Word (*sincerus amor verbi diuini, de Christo testantis, qui animum in scripturae tractatione occupatum tanta suauitate perfundet*). See J. J. Rambach, *Institutiones Hermeneuticae Sacrae* (Hartungian, 1725), 18.

ancient context of events . . . we must again learn to ask what claim or truth about man, his world, and transcendence we hear from these texts."[47]

Finally, the seminary as a text-community represents an instance of the Bible in context, and within the church it is an instance of the Bible in culture. The seminary is thus a test case for understanding texts in situations. As such, we maintain, the seminary's academic concerns provide the basis for its role in Ecclesia. It is by understanding text-in-situations that we can come to think rigorously about the application of the Bible to the needs of the Church.[48]

It is in these respects that we see the seminary making a significant contribution to Academia. We should emphasize that the seminary, as a part of Ecclesia, is "out of its realm" in Academia, but it nevertheless should continue to strive to participate in the task of Academia. We have argued above that the rationale for this lies in the nature of the seminary as a biblical text-community.

*The Academic Tasks of the Seminary*

The seminary has traditionally been involved in several areas of Academia. Here we want to evaluate the seminary's continual involvement in these areas in light of the previous discussion.

1) *Accreditation:* Accreditation is the seminary's primary link to Academia and as such is of central importance. It is by means of the standards of accreditation that the seminary measures its ability to live up to the responsibility to Academia discussed above. Accreditation is essential to a seminary because, for the most part, it involves precisely those aspects of the text-community which are most vulnerable to short range experiences, e.g., library facilities, quality faculty, academic freedom, the institution's conformity to its own standards

---

47 Peter Stuhlmacher, *Historical Criticism and Theological Interpretation of Scripture* (Fortress Press, 1977), 85. See also Peter Stuhlmacher, *Vom Verstehen des Neuen Testaments: Eine Hermeneutik* (Vandenhoeck & Ruprecht, 1979).

48 Here is where the study of "Text Theory" can be applied directly to the needs of the seminary and Church. Just as the study of linguistics and anthropology has greatly aided missions theory in recent decades, so Text Theory, the natural extension of both linguistics and anthropology, can and should play an important role in conceptualizing the nature of future problems (Cf. Schmidt, *Texttheorie*).

and ideals. Accreditation serves the text-community by insisting on the maintenance of just these features. Without the incentive of accreditation, it is not likely that these areas would always receive their due attention.

2) *Publications:* The University claims to be *universitas litterarum*—the whole of letters. The seminary's contribution to Academia, however, suggests that this exclusive claim of the University is short sighted. We contend that Academia is the true *universitas litterarum* and that both the University and the seminary, along with several other institutions, play an essential role in it. Thus, as a text-community, a primary task of the seminary's faculty is to contribute to the seminary's publications (*universitas litterarum*).

We are not now speaking of the *litterarum* addressed to the Ecclesia, as important as that is to the seminary. We have in mind rather the seminary's role in maintaining the presence of the Bible, as the Word of God (*verbo dei*), in the "mind-constructed world" of Academia. We are also not speaking here of publications which fall under the domain of the University as such, namely, the Bible, as the word of man (*verbo hominis*). Though such publications are important in their own right, they do not meet the requirements of the task we are now speaking of.

In the first section of this paper we suggested that the task of every member of the seminary is hermeneutical and practical in that it is the application of the text to a life setting. Here is a case in point. What could be more important and essential than contributing to and shaping the "mind-constructed world" of our generation? As we have attempted to argue above, there is a rationale, a responsibility, and a valid prospect for the seminary community to make this type of contribution to Academia.

3) *Disciplines and Departments:* We will discuss at more length the internal structure of a seminary faculty in the next section on Ecclesia. That structure, as we envision it, should be determined by the nature of the practical tasks assigned within the seminary community. Some tasks will relate more to Academia and others to Ecclesia and we believe this should be reflected in the departmental and disciplinary structure of the seminary. We hasten to add that these tasks are not distinguished as "theoretical and practical." We have already

argued that all tasks within the seminary are "practical," that is, they consist of the application of Scripture (hermeneutics) to specific areas of life. Thus, within the concept of a text-community, academic tasks are, in fact, practical. They consist of the application of specific texts to specific situations in life.

Here, however, it is important to say that the internal structuring of the seminary faculty departments should reflect the dual concerns of Academia and Ecclesia. We believe such a division of the faculty would have a greater advantage over the present schema based on subject matter, e.g., Old Testament, New Testament, Church History, Theology, Ethics, and Homiletics. The reason is that in a text-community, every department has the same subject matter, that is, the Scriptures, and the same theoretical role, that is, interpretation (hermeneutics). What then begins to emerge as truly distinctive in the task of the seminary is the audience or context being addressed. Thus, we propose a conceptualization of departments that is object-oriented, that is, one based on the object of study rather than the *subject matter*.

Such a conceptualization of departments within a seminary would not necessarily entail an actual restructuring of the faculty. It implies only that, in the final analysis, the faculty structure of the seminary should be marked in some way by such a distinction. Moreover, this distinction, however it may be implemented, does not entail a difference in faculty skills or abilities. Academia does not demand more ability or rigor than Ecclesia. The same level of skills is required for both. To clarify this point we need to explain our understanding of the notion of "Scholarship" and, particularly, how it relates to that of "Academia."

*The Nature of Scholarship within Academia and Ecclesia*

We suggest that the two concepts of Academia and Scholarship, though often merged and identified in ordinary language, are in fact two quite distinct ideas. We have earlier described Academia as the realm of the human sciences in which man is the measure of all things. Thus, Academia is a realm with a specific set of allegiances. As we understand it, the term "Scholarship" bears no inherent relationship to such a realm, but rather denotes the rigor, thoroughness, and excellence, with which the application of a task is carried out. In this sense, the concept of "Scholarship" is to be applied as an ideal to both Academia and Ecclesia. We all should strive for scholarship in both the realm of Academia and that of Ecclesia. We all also ought to be aware that it is possible to do shoddy, unscholarly work in both Academia and Ecclesia.

Such an ideal of scholarship (*scholaris*) is directly related to the textual nature of the seminary community. It is hardly without good reason that within Scripture itself the duties of the king (Deut 17:18), the prophet (Jer 36:2), and the high priest (Ezra 7:10–11), are those of the scholar, that is, reading and applying the Scriptures to life.[49] A community founded on a text cannot tolerate anything less than genuine scholarship in its leaders. Moreover, the degree to which a seminary's community practices scholarship in all its tasks is a measure of its faithfulness to its fundamental commitments to the text of Scripture.

*The Function of the Seminary Text-Community within the Ecclesia*

In the first section of this paper we argued that the proper context of the seminary is the Christian church, the Ecclesia. We need here only repeat that point. The seminary exists by and in behalf of the Ecclesia. That is its primary realm.

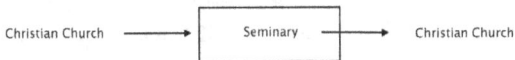

What remains for our purposes in this paper is to discuss the *tasks* of a seminary as a text-community within Ecclesia and the *skills* necessary to carry out those tasks.

---

49 See Deut 17:18 ("When the king sits upon the throne of his kingdom, he shall write for himself a copy of this Torah upon a book in the presence of the priests, the Levites; and it shall be with him so that he can read it all the days of his life so that he can learn to fear the Lord his God to keep all the words of this Torah and to do all its statues"), Jer 36:2 ("Take a scroll and write on it all the words I have spoken to you concerning Israel, Judah and all the other nations from the time I began speaking to you in the reign of Josiah till now..."), and Ezra 7:10-11 ("Ezra had determined to study diligently the Torah of the Lord and to do it and to teach its statutes and judgments in Israel").

## Part Two: The Tasks and Skills of a Seminary Text-Community

### Tasks and Disciplines

There are at least two ways to address the question of tasks. We could begin with the existing Academic disciplines, such as Old Testament, New Testament, etc., and the corresponding departments within the seminary and ask how these relate to the tasks of the seminary within Ecclesia. Or, we could begin with the tasks themselves and then ask either how the existing disciplines related to them or how the faculty could be redistributed to fit these tasks. We believe that the approach which allows for the greatest insight is the latter. Thus, that is the course we will follow in the remainder of this paper.

### Tasks and Domains

By "domains" we mean distinct areas or concrete social settings where specific tasks are defined and performed. Domains are distinguished by the specific "rules" and values which govern those who work within them. The seminary, for example, represents a domain within the realm of the ecclesia in that it is a socially realized setting within that realm. It has a clear set of fixed rules and values that distinguish it from other similar settings. A specific cultural context such as North America also represents a domain. Its rules and values are rooted in its social, cultural, and political structures.

What is helpful about the concept of domains is that they can be conceived of either as embedded within other domains or as intersecting with other domains. This allows flexibility in discussing the various tasks of each. When a domain is embedded in another they share the same rules, values, and tasks. When a domain intersects with another, its tasks and rules are determined by the other domain to the extent that they intersect. It accepts them, at least temporarily, as its own. A seminary in North America, for example, is embedded within a domain such as the cultural context of North America, but it can also intersect with another domain such as the cultural context of Africa. In doing so the seminary partially accepts the "rules" and values of the cultural context of Africa. Moreover, a seminary, as a domain, can be embedded within the church as a domain, or, more traditionally, it can merely intersect with the domain of the church.

The purpose of speaking of domains is two-fold. First, it provides a suitable context for speaking of tasks. We will define a task as an operation on or action within a domain. Second, the concept of a domain enables us to assign a relative value to a task. Tasks which relate to central domains of the seminary (as a text-community) are valued as central tasks. Tasks which relate to other domains are valued as peripheral. Such a hierarchy is invaluable when planning such structured strategies as curricula. The central domains of the seminary are listed in the following chart.

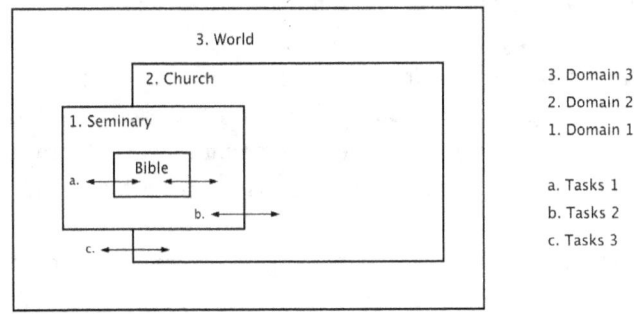

Domains and Tasks

We have listed here the domains which we believe are relevant and central to the text-community of the seminary. Along with these domains, we will discuss the tasks that relate to each domain and, as well, attempt to identify the necessary skills related to these tasks.

Along the way we will discuss the implications for adjustments in the seminary's structure to accommodate these tasks.

## Domain 1: The Seminary Text-Community

The first domain is that of the seminary text-community itself. As a biblical text-community, the seminary is a domain that has embedded within it yet another domain, that is, the world of the biblical text. We are using the concept of an embedded domain as defined above, namely, both the seminary and the world of the biblical text share the same set of rules and values.

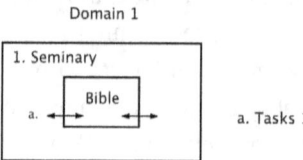

The primary tasks within this domain are those which relate to "reading" the text and "steering" the community so that they *continue* to maintain and obey the same rules and values. It is by means of this task that the seminary, as a community, remains biblical. We are not thinking here of "reading" the text simply as attempting to get at the sense of the text in a static, or once and for all manner. Though that is obviously one of the tasks of a seminary, we have in mind, rather, the analogy of navigation in which the "reading" of one's instruments (the Bible) is relative to a ship's (the seminary) present location at sea. Thus the "reading" which is here applied to the text is one that has already "located" the position of the text-community and is prepared to make necessary adjustments to its course which are suggested by each new reading.

The skills necessary for such a reading of the text are clearly multifarious. One must be at home both in the world of the text and the seminary community.[50] The primary focus of the two sets of skills is on the point where they intersect. Curiously enough, it could be argued that a specific skill that comes closest to this point of intersection is that of "textual criticism." Traditionally, this has been the most arcane of all the arcane concerns of biblical scholars. This is because the object of textual criticism has most frequently been understood as the establishment of the "correct text."

As worthy a goal as that is, it overlooks the fact that all of those "secondary readings" which litter the apparatus of the critical edition of the Bible are, in fact, priceless relics and traces of the ages-long rubbing of the biblical text against its constantly shifting context—the life of the Christian (and Jewish) communities. Uncovering such

---

50 The "world of the text" as we understand it, is the "world making" capacity of the biblical texts themselves. Texts such as the Bible do more than import information. They, in fact, construe a world that presents itself to the reader as reality. In the case of the Bible, this reality is, in fact, true.

traces is equivalent to the anthropologist's study of early human remains. They tell us who we are because they show us where we came from and how we got where we are.

For the most part, the skills necessary at this level are quite different than those which faculty members are prepared for in graduate school. They are inter-disciplinary, or better, trans-disciplinary. To carry through with the analogy of navigation, for example, the skills one usually learns in graduate school for biblical exegesis are comparable to those of a coast guard crew examining a ship at sea. When they board the ship, the coast guard solicits from the ship's crew the location of the ship (its coordinates) when it left port, the time it left, and its original destination. Based on such information the coast guard crew is required to make a judgment on the ship's location and cargo relative to its original location and destination. How did it get to its present location? Is it off its original course? How far is it from its port? Or its destination?

The skills required for the tasks of biblical exegesis in a text-community, on the other hand, are those that the crew of the ship itself are required to have which enable them to chart the sea to arrive at their destination. It is one thing to know how the ship got to its present location; it is another thing to know how to get it there or how to get it to some other destination.

The analogy is a helpful one because it shows that the skills of the two crews differ most in the fact that the one set of skills is static and the other is dynamic. The coast guard crew makes its evaluation based on the *original location* of the ship, whereas the crew of the ship itself not only needs that information but it must also take constant readings of their continually changing location as well as of their instruments and make appropriate adjustments.

The point of this analogy is to show that it is not enough to read the Bible in its original context. As important, and essential as that is, more is required. The Bible must be read continuously in its ongoing context, and, in Tasks level 1, that context is the seminary community.

It is important here to make it clear that the context we have in mind at this point is *that of the seminary* as a text-generated community. We are not yet speaking of the further domains listed below, that is, the seminary within the church and within the world. In our opinion, it would be a major oversight for the seminary curriculum to attempt (at this level) to teach students to read the biblical text in light of such wider domains in the church and the world. Here we are speaking only of the relationship between the seminary and its embedded biblical text-world. How does the biblical text shape the seminary community itself? And, How is the biblical text shaped by that same community?

This is a crucial, and often overlooked, aspect of the tasks of the seminary curriculum. At strategic points along the way, the seminary's curriculum should focus on and speak to the personal life of the members of the seminary community itself. The student and the faculty administration should consciously and intentionally address the question, What does this (the Bible) mean to me and my family *now while I am in seminary*? What we are suggesting is that this is not a peripheral question. Given the seminary's identity as a textual community it is a central question that should be addressed by the shape and content of the curriculum itself.

At the same time we are aware that the seminary is a part of the larger community of the church, and the church is a part of the world. Thus, an ability to read the text in light of the seminary community entails an awareness of the embedded nature of that community (see discussion below). At this point, however, we want to put a clear emphasis on the importance of the seminary itself as a text-community and the responsibility of the seminary to itself. The reservoir from which a life of ministry draws is filled and nourished by the prayerful study of God's Word.

*Levels of Skills—Scholarship*

What level of skills are necessary to carry out this task of reading the text and locating the community? We suggest that the requirement of "scholarship" set the standard for the nature and level of skills to carry out this task. We also suggest that the same level of skills be required on all sides. That is, the "reading" of the text should be done with the same level of expertise as that of "locating" the community. The ability to work with the original biblical language is as essential as sensitivity to culture.

## Effects of Tasks and Skills

What is the desired effect of the tasks and skills envisioned within this domain? The aim or goal is simply to keep the seminary community in line with the "rules" and values of the biblical text. By "rules" and values we mean the ideals and standards intended and taught by the authors of the biblical texts. We include in this, of course, the whole notion of the "mind constructed world" of the text which is spoken of above. The centrality of this domain to the nature of the seminary as a text-community means that the tasks envisioned here are central tasks to ministry.

## Implementation of Tasks 1 within a Seminary

When viewed from the perspective of the existing structure of a seminary, one can see that there is no single department having the necessary skills to carry out these tasks. One might think of the Missions Department as a starting point since it already has "cross-cultural" skills up and running. The problem with such skills, however, is that they relate to other types of domains, such as the intersection of the church and the world.

The domains we have in mind are much more closely defined. They relate most closely to the traditional tasks of "Dogmatics" (or Doctrine) as distinguished from "Systematic Theology," that is, teaching the community of faith to live by the standard of God's Word. The biblical studies departments have the requisite linguistic skills, but not the "navigational skills" necessary to read the present location of the seminary's community. Moreover, in many seminaries these departments have heavily invested in skills directed toward deriving static information from the biblical texts.

## Target Audience: The Seminary Community Itself?

One of the reasons the seminary is ill prepared for these tasks which relate to the seminary itself as a community is that this specific domain is most often overlooked in favor of a focus on the domain of the church. The seminary itself is not identified as a specific kind of community, but merely as an appendage to the church. We suggest that when viewed, not as a text-community in its own right but merely as an appendage to the church, the seminary is forced to focus its tasks first and foremost on the tasks of the church.

This is the genesis and common justification of the notion that the seminary is a professional school, whose task it is to teach the necessary skills of running a church. We are not here attempting to question the merits of such a view of the seminary. We are rather attempting to show that even when such an approach to the nature and purpose of a seminary is taken, failing to recognize the place of the seminary as a community within that purpose is a major oversight.

It is just such an oversight which gives the seminary community a lingering sense that a more basic need of students is not being met by such a program. Evidence of this sense of need, we believe, can be seen in the frequent ad hoc attempts at "spiritual formation" and the belief that the cure-all for what ails students is the addition of this or that course to the required curriculum.[51] Thus seminaries add courses on prayer, worship, evangelism—features of the biblical text-world that should be a natural part of the seminary community and thus at the center of the purpose of the curriculum. By overlooking the seminary's fundamental tasks of locating and maintaining *itself* as an authentic text-community, the seminary is left without a real platform from which to launch its own further assault on such domains as the church and the world.

If we are correct in our assessment of the seminary as a text-community and if it is true that this aspect of the seminary has rarely been addressed by the seminary itself, the question of what to do about it naturally arises. We suggest the following: First, we have to acknowledge that this domain and the tasks it entails is central to the seminary as such. There is really no more basic feature of the seminary itself. Second, if this is in fact a central, defining, concern of the seminary then it makes sense that the structure of the seminary should also reflect it.

---

51 I wrote this paragraph over a year ago, long before I had any knowledge of the nature of the new curriculum at DTS. I have left this sentence intact because it honestly reflects my thoughts, though I realize it could be misread as a statement against the new DTS curriculum. Please don't read it that way.

## Seminary Faculty Structure

As we have already suggested, the traditional division of the faculty into departments based on subject matter (e.g., Old Testament, New Testament, etc), may not be the most efficient alignment of faculty resources. It is possible, and perhaps desirable, to replace it with a division of faculty along lines that reflect various Tasks of the seminary as well as the text-in-situation nature of the seminary itself. In other words, at the level of Tasks 1 skills, there could be a department or task group made up of a segment of faculty whose primary responsibilities are directed toward the development of the seminary student within the context of the seminary. What I have in mind is something that has frequently been a part of the Bible School tradition, that is, a group of faculty (designated or not designated as such) and courses (designated or not designated as such) that focus on basic Christian Life issues.

The aim and goal would be an intentional development *in the seminary student* of such qualities as Christian character and maturity, godly living, a strong marriage and family, as well as basic Bible knowledge and doctrine. The important point is not the subject matter of the courses but their goal, that is, developing the skills of working with the biblical text in context, specifically, the student's own context of the seminary community. For example, the focus of such classes would not be "how to prepare a sermon from this or that biblical text" but rather "how to live and act biblically," or "how does a father or mother teach their children to love God and obey Him?"

These are practical skills in biblical hermeneutics which are directed at the student during the time he or she is a part of the seminary community itself. A question such as "preaching from the Old Testament" would belong in the context of another domain, the church, though it would build on the present domain. Before attempting to preach to others, we believe the student should know how to live biblically and apply Scripture to his or her own life and family within their present situation at seminary.

It is, of course, not necessary to break up the existing departments to achieve this purpose. Individual faculty members could merely be designated to specific tasks, or those tasks could be rotated throughout the departments. It would be valuable, however, if some organizational structure were given to the faculties so designated as it would provide the opportunity for planning courses and evaluating their effectiveness.

*Seminary Curriculum Structure for Tasks 1*

Whatever the actual departmental structure, we suggest that at this level curriculum be arranged around three primary areas of concern: 1) Exegesis or, Bible Content; 2) Dogmatics, or Doctrine; and 3) Devotion, or Christian Life. The chart below shows these three areas of focus in the curriculum and their target in the seminary community.

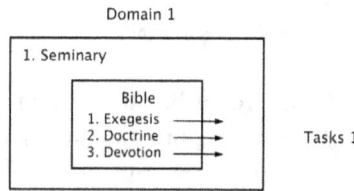

If we take seriously the priority of the structure suggested above, then the actual courses developed to implement this structure would also be affected. For example, the first set of skills, Exegesis or, Bible Content, need not be divided along departmental lines, that is, Old Testament and New Testament. Since the primary focus of the courses is the integration of the Bible into the life setting of the student (which is a question of canon), such a focus already entails the integration of the Old Testament and the New, which is also a question of canon. It thus would make sense to treat both of these aspects of canon within the same context.

*The Effect of Curriculum Focus on the Seminary*

The effect of such a focus would be two-fold. First, it would go a long way toward building and sustaining a biblical seminary community. A strong and vital community would have a further effect on its own members. The role of the social context in shaping and helping to internalize ideals and values is well known. Such a cohesive community becomes all the more important in the context of an increasingly scattered student population (e.g., block scheduling, part-time students, and extension courses). Second, the internal focus of the curriculum on the seminary community itself would greatly aid in the introduction of basic concepts of relating texts to real life situations. At a further level within the seminary curriculum, these same skills can then be extended to other domains such as the church and the world.

*Multiple Track ThM Curriculum*

Sooner or later in a text-community the question of the biblical languages arises. As we see it, there are, at least, five model curricula with respect to the role of the biblical languages. We will briefly describe each model and discuss its pros and cons. We will not attempt to give a justification for any of the models.

*Two Degree Program*

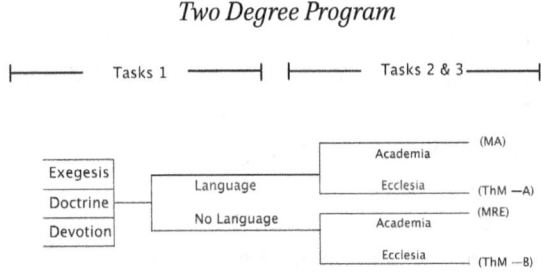

It is possible to eliminate the language requirements for a portion of the students who take the ThM degree. This would have the effect of freeing credit hours, allowing more concentration in other areas. The end result would produce two, distinct ThM degrees. These could be marked in some way to indicate that one entailed the biblical languages and the other did not (ThM-A, ThM-B); or the degree could be integrated into a "major" or specialization program in which a segment of the "majors" (ThM-A, ThM-B) required the biblical languages.

The obvious drawback to such a plan is that it would require a duplication of a large part of the faculty for tasks at all levels. Certainly at the level of Tasks 1, the entire program would have to be offered in duplicate, one set of courses which is built on the biblical languages and another which is not.

*Two Track Program*

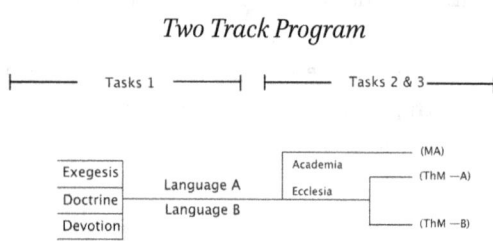

The idea of this model is that the biblical languages can be taught at more than one level. The languages can be taught as such (Language A), or use of the language tools (lexicons, grammars, commentaries) can be taught with only bare essentials of the language itself (Language B).

Even if it were possible to accomplish the intended objectives of this model (that is, use of the tools without knowledge of the language itself), it would suffer the same drawbacks as the two degree program. That is, it would require large scale duplication of faculty and courses at the Tasks 1 level.

A more fundamental problem with this approach, however, is related to the textual nature of the seminary and the Christian church, discussed throughout this paper. The subtleties of the use of a language in texts and the communities generated by them is such that a use of "tools" in a foreign language is not likely to help grasp its meaning in texts. Given the textual nature of the Christian church and the central role of translations (English) in it, there is more value in the Two Degree program discussed above which, at least, would allow practice in relating understandable texts (albeit translations) to real life situations. The fact that in the Protestant church, at least, translations of the Bible have always been understood as "translations" and only valid in so far as they represent the original, means that this also would not be a desirable approach to curriculum.

## Common Denominator Program

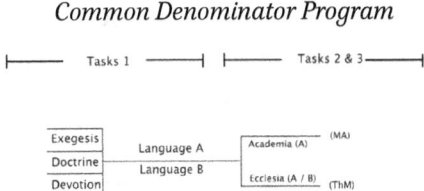

This model is a variation on the two-track program discussed above. It recognizes that the faculty manpower required to run a genuine two-track program is prohibitive. It thus runs both Language-A and Language-B students through the same set of courses. The courses are then calibrated to the Language-B students.

The obvious drawback of this approach is what it does to the ThM Language-A students. It leaves them with little actual practice in applying their knowledge of the language to Tasks 1 skills. Moreover, Language-A students would already know how to use the language tools, since that would be a feature of learning the language.

Furthermore, this approach contains the same fundamental problem as the two-track approach mentioned above. The subtleties of the use of language in texts and the communities generated by them is such that a use of "tools" in a foreign language is not likely to help grasp its meaning in texts.

## One Track Program

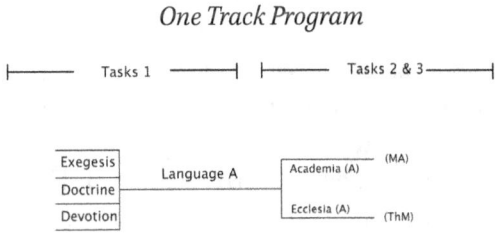

The model of requiring all students to study the Bible on the basis of the original languages has the obvious advantage of keeping the curriculum focused and limiting the size of the faculty.

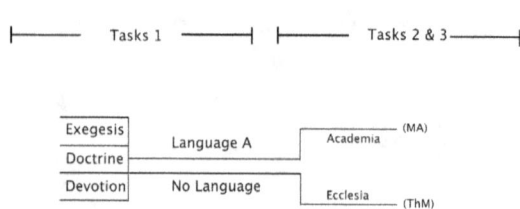

Like several of the other models listed above, the Translation-Only approach to the ThM calls for additional faculty to handle duplication within the Tasks 1 level courses. In effect, such a program would create a separate, and isolated set of Academia courses. Moreover, a heavy concentration of faculty time (i.e., teaching biblical languages and related courses) would go into the relatively less central realm of Academia.

*The Setting of Tasks 1*

By the nature of the case, that is, given the importance of a text-community, the setting of courses at this level should be, primarily, the seminary campus.

## Domain 2: The Seminary Text-Community within the Christian Church

We have discussed earlier the nature of the seminary as a text-community formed by and in behalf of the church. The seminary is thus a domain embedded within or intersecting with the domain of the church. As such there is another level of tasks to which it is obliged. In the discussion which follows we will attempt to define and describe these tasks, and their requisite skills, as aspects of the textual nature of both the seminary and the church. Just as the first level of tasks involved the skill of reading the Bible and the community, so this level involves reading the Bible and the church.

*The Seminary and the Church*

There are at least two possible models of the seminary in relationship to the church. In the first, the seminary is embedded within the domain of the church and in the second it intersects with it.

### The Mega-Church Model

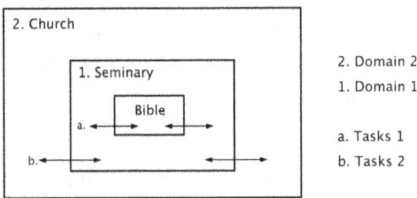

With the existence of mega-church congregations financially capable of maintaining a small faculty, the prospect of a seminary embedded in a local church is a real one today. For a number of reasons, without actually listing them here, we suggest that such an arrangement is not practical or preferable for the seminary at large. We would agree, however, that there is a place for such limited range seminaries.

In the discussion which follows, we will view the relationship between the seminary and the church as one that intersects. That is, it does not share the same rules but rather accepts the rules of the church as its own while not forsaking its own rules.

Examples of seminary rules include such items as exams, papers, projects, courses, calendar, pass/fail requirements, and degrees. It should be obvious that such rules differ from typical church "rules" such as sacraments, discipline, oversight of elders, and acceptance.

### The Seminary Intersecting the Church Model

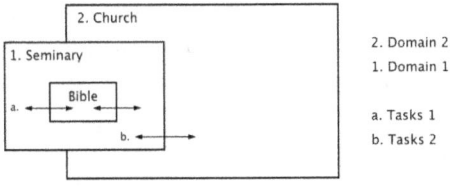

We believe the model of a seminary intersecting with the church rather than embedded in it is not only more flexible but also provides a wider base for fulfilling the seminary's legitimate commitments to other realms, such as Academia.

*Skills of Tasks 2 Applied to the Church*

The primary tasks of the seminary in the domain of the church is to train church leaders who are able to create, sustain, and nourish the church as a text-community.

Put simply, the focus of the skills at this level is the ability to read the Scriptures in light of the church community and the ability to guide the church in living according to the light of the Scriptures. In view of the seminary model proposed in this paper, this means that the scriptural "reading" skills developed in Tasks 1 can now be implemented and applied at the level of Tasks 2. Thus, the primary new skills to be learned and developed at this level are those of "reading" the church community.

*Implementation of Skills and Tasks*

For the most part, the faculty departments and courses which focus on these skills are already in place in the seminary. The primary tasks are then, first, providing a suitable link with Tasks 1 so that skills learned and practiced at that level can be further developed within the church community; and, second, providing real-life situations within which to practice these skills.

*Tasks 1 Links to Tasks 2*

Corresponding to the three main areas of concern is the structure of the curriculum suggested for Tasks 1, we suggest the following three areas of concern for Tasks 2: 1) Homiletics, 2) Christian Education, and 3) Pastoral Ministries.

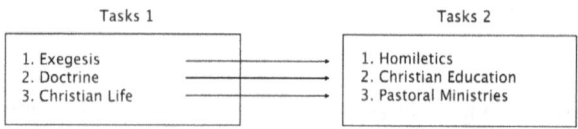

## The Setting of Tasks 2

The "text-in-context" nature of the seminary's tasks, which has been stressed throughout this paper, makes it obvious that this stage of the seminary's curriculum should be carried out as much as possible within the context of the church itself. Here is where the intersecting nature of the relationship of the seminary and the church is helpful. Ultimately, the rules of the game are those of the seminary. The goal of the instruction, however, should always be the rules of the church. What we mean by this is that insofar as it is logistically possible, the seminary student should do the actual work of the church as the major part of his or her studies at this level, but the evaluation of it should come from the side of the seminary faculty.

This obviously requires a great deal of cooperation from the church in providing sufficient opportunity for learning. If present experiences with internships and/or apprenticeships are any guide, we will no doubt have to develop new and different means for implementing this kind of instruction. Not only can we not expect the time commitment from pastors and church leaders required in the internship style programs, but more importantly, the lack of control and level of instruction which internships inevitably entail make it suitable for only a part of this level of seminary instruction. Something different is needed for the central framework.

We would like to suggest three avenues by which Tasks 2 level skills can be developed within actual ministry situations. This is an area that obviously needs more thought and much organization. Moreover, there are cost limitations. In any event, working with Tasks 2 skills in actual ministry situations is an ideal that should govern curriculum planning at this level.

### 1) Strategic Use of Technology

It is just at this level (Tasks 2), and not earlier (Tasks 1), that recent (and no doubt future) developments in technology can be applied to assist the instructional value and evaluation of the student in on-site learning. Some technologies are already in place which have not yet been implemented by the seminary. The "mini-cam" set on a tripod in the back of the church during an actual sermon, for example, makes the homiletics lab all but obsolete. Conference calls, computer modems, and/or a fax machine, can link a national or international "classroom" session in which a single professor can conduct a regular course schedule with students actively involved in actual ministries throughout the world. It is thus already technologically possible to conduct a regular course or seminar with students involved in active ministry. Similar conferences are being held in the business world every day.

Moreover, in the near future, such communication links will be possible not only by voice and computer screen but through a video screen as well. In my opinion, the seminary should already be developing the courses for such eventualities. We are not suggesting that these courses will dominate the seminary's overall curriculum, but rather that they provide the precise means for implementing the on-site requirements of Tasks 2 skills. By adding such procedures to the already successful modular courses, it is not unrealistic even at the present time to plan a segment of the seminary curriculum around the concept of on-site learning as a major component of the level of Tasks 2.

It should be stressed here that the goal of courses at this level would not be "instructional" as such, but rather, "evaluative" and "reflective" of actual ministry experience. As we envision it, the student could prearrange a ministry setting (as part of his or her application to seminary) with a home church or para-church organization, or (after completion of the level of Tasks 1) seek it through the internship/placement office. This setting would then provide the laboratory for the development of Tasks 2 level skills. After completion of Tasks 1 level courses and initial Tasks 2 (and 3) courses, the student could complete the remainder of the Tasks 2 (and 3) level courses in a ministry setting.

*2) Mini-Conference/Seminar Format*

The nature of all Tasks 2 courses should be such that they could be taught on campus or on a modular basis at a distant location. To facilitate the student's opportunities for on-site learning, these courses should be as transportable as possible. An idea that has been extensively developed in the sales and marketing world is the mini-conference and seminar, usually held at an airport hotel in a major or centrally located city. It is not hard to imagine Tasks 2 level courses developed for a series of two-day conferences at a centrally located hotel for students already involved in ministry. Students who have completed Tasks 1 and initial Tasks 2 (and 3) could begin a ministry situation and continue their Tasks 2 (and 3) level courses, at least in part, at such seminars. These would have the advantage of face-to-face contact with a professor, and would thus augment the other kinds of technology-based instruction and interaction discussed above. There are other advantages to such an arrangement which we will not discuss here (e.g., focus, concentration, flexibility, adjustability, and modifiability).

### 3) Partnerships with Mega-Churches

Another possibility for implementing on-site learning of Tasks 2 skills is the establishment of partnership agreements with existing mega-churches. If the mega-church phenomena survives in the 2000s, it will require a steady stream of trained leaders. Though they may not yet see the light, the textual nature of these mega-communities will mandate that they provide their leaders with Tasks 1 level skills. It will surely be impractical for these churches to attempt such training on their own and they will have to seek help. The seminary has what they will need. Moreover, these mega-church communities also have what the seminary needs—students and ministry opportunities. It thus seems reasonable that the seminary should enter into partnerships with such churches whereby through our Tasks 1–3 curriculum, we could help train their own leaders.

There are several additional advantages to the concept of on-site learning of Tasks 2 skills.

### 1) Continuing Education

In such an environment, the idea of continuing education becomes a natural consequence of seminary education as an on-going part of ministry. If the skills of the ministry are initially developed within an actual ministry setting, the prospect of continuing the development of those skills after graduation and of adding new skills is just as realistic as the work done on the original degree itself.

*2) Degree Updates*

Given the flexibility of on-site learning which we are suggesting here, the notion of a seminary degree itself receives new vitality. Within such a framework, it is not hard to envision the development of a concept of a degree "update" whereby a ThM earned five, ten, or 15 years earlier can be augmented by the same systems developed for the degree itself. The rapidly changing modes of thinking and culture *within the church* itself would make an on-going update of one's degree almost mandatory.

*3) ThM links to DMin*

Such "updates" of a ThM degree could also be preliminary and prerequisite for work on a DMin and hence add further meaning and value to it. If such an on-going update and review schedule were locked on to the DMin, it would provide a desperately needed gauge for its credibility as a professional degree.

DOMAIN 3: THE CHURCH WITHIN THE WORLD
(INTERSECTING WITH CULTURE)

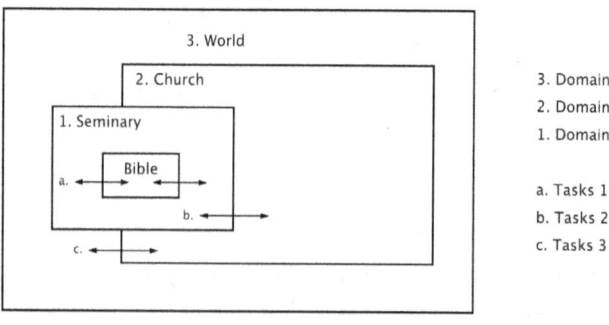

## The Nature and Function of Tasks 3 in a Seminary Text-Community

The sequence of tasks from Tasks 1 to Tasks 3 is a logical, not a temporal, one. This means that already at the level of Tasks 1 and Tasks 2 the questions of Tasks 3 can and should be raised. The seminary is a part of the world and the church is a part of the world. Thus, there is a legitimate place for the development of Tasks 3 skills within the framework of both Tasks 1 and Tasks 2.

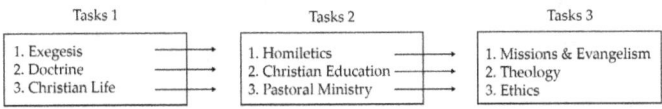

In light of the role of the seminary as a text-community formed by and in behalf of the church, however, the primary focus of Tasks 3 level skills should be at the Tasks 2 level.

The primary question, then, is "How does the church relate to the world?"

2

# The Seminary as a Textual Community: Reflections on John Sailhamer's Vision for Theological Education

*Ched Spellman and Jason K. Lee*

WHAT IS THE PURPOSE OF A SEMINARY? Because of financial pressures and the shifting mores of higher education, those training for ministry today have become less tolerant of lengthy degree programs and loosely connected coursework. A prevailing question among potential students continues to be, "Is a seminary education worth the cost?" In this scenario, the coherence of a seminary's vision for theological education and the integrated nature of their course of study is a paramount concern.

John Sailhamer (1946–2017) is known for his careful scholarship on the Hebrew Bible and his focus on the compositional strategies found in the text of Scripture. Perhaps less well-known is his vision for theological education. In "The Nature, Purpose, and Tasks of a Theological Seminary," Sailhamer articulates a comprehensive vision for theological education that is worth considering. In this essay, we will outline the circumstances that led to this address, discuss the main lines of Sailhamer's argument, and then consider some of the central themes of the address and their relevance for contemporary educators.

SETTING: ENVISIONING THE TASK OF THEOLOGICAL EDUCATION

In 1993, there was a transition in the leadership structure of Dallas Theological Seminary (DTS). After eight years of serving as president of the school, Donald K. Campbell decided to retire. In 1994, Chuck Swindoll became the fourth president of DTS. The initial plan for the administration of the school was for Swindoll to remain in California where the church and ministry he was leading was located. In this scenario with the president providing leadership from out of state, the position of provost was to handle the day-to-day workings of the school and shape the academic curriculum. In mid-1993, John Sailhamer was selected to fill this role.[1] He left his teaching position at Trinity Evangelical Divinity School at the end of the Spring semester and prepared to begin leading at DTS.

When Swindoll reflects on his journey to DTS, he also notes the nature of this leadership structure. He recounts in a book published this same year, "It will be an unusual arrangement (another of the Spirit's many surprises), whereby I will remain a pastor of a local church, yet still be free to provide the vision, direction, and motivation for the seminary." "My plan," Swindoll continues, "is to be on hand as much as possible through the year to touch and influence the lives of those in training for a lifetime of ministry. And because of the gifts, diligence, willingness, and competence of the man who will come aboard with me as the provost of the school—Dr. John Sailhamer—I will not have to concern myself with all the time-consuming and energy-draining details that normally sap the strength and blur the vision of a school's president."[2] Sailhamer echoes this understanding of the leadership arrangement, stating that Swindoll would be "like the ground control, giving instructions, suggestions, and directions for the flight" and that he would "serve as the pilot, making sure those directions were carried out, the passengers were taken care of, and the destination reached."[3]

---

[1] The announcement that Swindoll would be appointed president with Sailhamer as provost was broadly circulated in the Summer of 1993. For example, see the notice in *The Baptist Record* of the Mississippi Baptist Convention (June 17, 1993), 6. On the transition to Swindoll as president of the school, see also John D. Hannah, *An Uncommon Union: Dallas Theological Seminary and American Evangelicalism* (Zondervan, 2009), 227–256 ("The Restabilization of the Seminary in Mainstream Evangelicalism: The Swindoll Presidency, 1994–2001").

[2] Charles R. Swindoll, *Flying Closer to the Flame: A Passion for the Holy Spirit* (Word Publishers, 1993), 93–94. Written with his transition to DTS in view, Swindoll also dedicates the volume to Donald K. Campbell whom he notes is finishing his tenure at the school. Swindoll states that this opportunity is "one of the greatest surprises" of his life (93).

[3] Swindoll himself conveyed this analogy from Sailhamer in a letter to his church in California about the new position at DTS (see "A Personal Letter to the Fullerton

As the presidential transition developed, it became evident that Swindoll would move his ministry to Texas and take a more active role in the day-to-day operations of the seminary. In light of some of these changes in the leadership structure and other factors, Sailhamer decided not to accept the role of provost at DTS and resigned the position.[4] When Swindoll was inaugurated president in 1994, he restructured the DTS administration in part by omitting the provost position and becoming more involved in the business of the school as a resident president.[5] After several years of writing and teaching at various institutions, Sailhamer went on to serve as professor of Old Testament and Hebrew at Southeastern Baptist Theological Seminary in 1999.[6]

In the Spring and Summer of 1993, then, Sailhamer prepared for this possible role of provost by articulating a vision for theological education and its possible implementation at a seminary like DTS. Though he ended up not taking this position, his address represents what he saw as an ideal arrangement of the school's faculty, curriculum, and institutional priorities. While unpublished, the address is a completed work that was intended for public delivery. This document therefore stands as an important historical artifact from a transitional time in the history of DTS and also as a developed blueprint for the teaching philosophy that Sailhamer worked out across his career as an educator.

---

Flock from Pastor Chuck Swindoll," as quoted in Hannah, *Uncommon Union*, 233).

4 On the decision to transition from DTS, see Patty Sailhamer, "Biography of John H. Sailhamer," in *Text and Canon: Essays in Honor of John H. Sailhamer* (Pickwick Publications, 2017), xi–xvi. She recounts that "by the end of 1993, Swindoll had decided to move to Dallas. His hopes were that John would agree to stay on as provost and assist him for the next decade at DTS. After due consideration, John decided he would best serve by continuing to teach and he withdrew from the plan to become provost. Still, he had already resigned from Trinity and felt that chapter of his life was closed" (xiv).

5 On this administrative reorganization at DTS, see "Chuck Swindoll Named Next President of Dallas Seminary," *Kindred Spirit* 17 (May–August 1993): 9; "Charles Swindoll Names New Leadership Team," *Kindred Spirit* 18 (May–August 1994): 8; and Hannah, *Uncommon Union*, 233–236.

6 See "Renowned Hebrew scholar to join Southeastern Seminary's faculty," *Baptist Press* (April 19, 1999).

## Substance: Crafting the Coherence of a Seminary Curriculum

An overview of the structure and emphasis of this address will help orient further reflection on its significance and possible value. As he begins, Sailhamer describes the problems he seeks to take up and signals the direction he will begin to develop. From his perspective, "present seminary programs at best often lack a cohesive center and are otherwise often incoherent or, in some cases, irrational." His purpose is to "provide a theoretical and reflective basis for designing a coherent and cohesive curriculum (both explicit and implicit)." This abstract and theoretical discussion is necessary for evangelicals because the purpose of theological education is rooted in revealed truth. Ensuring that each aspect of ministry training is explicitly or implicitly grounded in the Scriptures and undertaken for the sake of the churches is an urgent and necessary endeavor. For Sailhamer, this practical and theoretical requirement warrants an extended reflection on the nature, purpose, and tasks of a theological seminary.

In part one, Sailhamer outlines his understanding of the *nature* and *purpose* of a seminary. In an evangelical institution, one must think carefully about the relationship of the seminary to the Christian churches and also the seminary to the Christian Scriptures. Accordingly, the purpose of a seminary is "to glorify the Living Word of God who is known in the written Word of God" and it does this "specifically by preparing ministers of the Word." Having established this all-important theological and hermeneutical foundation, Sailhamer then discusses the relationship between the seminary and the academy. Carefully distinguishing and relating the church and the academy enables the seminary to maintain its distinctive role in relation to both domains.

Because of its non-negotiable theological commitments, the seminary offers something the university is not able to provide. "As a matter of fact," Sailhamer explains, "a proper study of the Bible as an object within the [academy] can only be appreciated and carried out within the context of a text-community such as a theological seminary." Having established the necessity of both the academy and the church, Sailhamer next discusses the academic tasks that are necessary for a seminary to function properly. These include achieving and maintaining accreditation, producing scholarly publications, and contributing to academic disciplines with an integrated faculty structure.

In part two, Sailhamer considers and articulates the tasks and skills that would undergird this brand of theological education. In order to guide this discussion of tasks and skills, Sailhamer orients his comments around the concept of "domains." The major domains relevant to this discussion are the seminary, the church, and the world. Specific tasks that are appropriate for each of these domains can then be developed. Because of the way these domains overlap to an extent in an evangelical context, a given task may serve multiple domains. This orientation also allows a seminary to prioritize certain tasks (e.g., exegesis) that might be secondary in other domains (e.g., engaging culture).

The final section of the address provides a working outline of what a curriculum with this set of values and administrative priorities might look like. Sailhamer considers some logistical questions about the role of biblical languages in a ThM degree and the implications each scenario would likely have in relation to the overarching goals of the program of study. He does this analysis with respect to the domain of the seminary community itself and also as the seminary community finds itself within the domain of the Christian churches. Depending on the structure of the ecclesial community, the logistics of theological education would look different. Here Sailhamer considers such elements as the use of technology, the priority of on-site training, and also the type of degrees that would complement and serve these church communities.

Sailhamer concludes his address by briefly considering the domain of the world and how the church intersects with culture. Here, he postures toward the relationship of the seminary context and the church community to the tasks of missions, evangelism, theology, and ethics. His final words in the address ask the question, "How does the church relate to the world?" These last sections of his address are the most technical in part because he is considering how the foundation for theological education articulated in the first parts of the address would inform an actual curricular journey in a school like DTS or in a given local church context. His work in these final sections of his address, then, can be viewed as a working model for the type of curriculum that might complement his overarching vision.

## Significance: Reflecting on the Strategic Value of this Vision for Theological Education

In addition to its significance as a historical document and as a revealing part of Sailhamer's philosophy of academic ministry, several of the central themes of this address have an enduring value for contemporary theological education. These emphases have considerable explanatory power in their own right, and when combined within an overarching model for academic ministry can have a formative influence on any seminary context.

### Defining the Seminary as a Textual Community

Perhaps one of the most distinctive aspects of Sailhamer's address is his identification of the seminary as a textual community. The seminary's purposes ("Tasks") and spheres of ministry ("Domains") are established by its core identity as a text-community and the nature of the biblical text that produces and guides it. In his address, Sailhamer characterizes a "textual community" as one that "conceptualizes its own existence in terms of authoritative texts."[7] He reflects further, "As a biblical text-community, the seminary is a domain that has embedded within it yet another domain, that is, the world of the biblical text" meaning that "both

---

7 In his section on "The Seminary and the Scriptures," Sailhamer also draws upon Kevin Vanhoozer's definition of a textual community as a "community united by, indeed constituted by, a foundational text—the Christian Scriptures." Sailhamer develops this notion by arguing that "the role of the Scriptures as texts in the seminary community is more than a means of conceptualizing its Christian identity, it is, as well, constitutive of the seminary community itself." Though the possible nuances between a "text-community" and a "textual community" are worth pursuing, in this essay these descriptions are used interchangeably. On the use of this concept from a different angle in the study of literacy and manuscript cultures in the ancient and medieval eras, see Jane Heath, "'Textual Communities': Brian Stock's Concept and Recent Scholarship on Antiquity," in *Scriptural Interpretation at the Interface between Education and Religion*, ed. Florian Wilk (Brill, 2018), 5–35. Heath broadly characterizes a textual community as "a community whose life, thought, sense of identity and relations with outsiders are organised around an authoritative text" (5).

the seminary and the world of the biblical text share the same set of rules and values." Recognizing the biblical canon as an authoritative text will shape the makeup of the faculty, the student body, and the curriculum. Both the seminary's vision and its activities will be guided by its commitment to being a biblical text-community.

As the text-community of a seminary is of first importance to Sailhamer's vision, the execution of such a vision requires a dynamic reading of the biblical text "in its ongoing context . . . the seminary community." This version of communal reading is not unmoored from a sound interpretative approach (see below), but it does "put a clear emphasis on the importance of the seminary itself as a text-community and the responsibility of the seminary to itself." For students and faculty alike, this recognition of the seminary as a text-community creates the atmosphere of communal submission to the authoritative biblical text. The formative features of this text-community affect not only a student's future ministry but also shapes his or her present ministry within the seminary context. This vision means that the current seminary context actualizes ministry activity in service to the text and in keeping with the implied faith response on the part of its readers. Sailhamer contends that viewing the seminary as a text-community is essential because the "reservoir from which a life of ministry draws is filled and nourished by the prayerful study of God's Word."

Without focusing on the seminary as a text-community, this domain can be diminished inadvertently by those who rightly focus on the local church. In this case, the "seminary itself is not identified as a specific kind of community, but merely as an appendage to the church." From this flawed perspective, crucial elements of seminary life—those of a text-community—are neglected. Sailhamer laments that failing to recognize the seminary as its own textual community is a "major oversight" of many theological schools and seminaries. Furthermore, when the seminary is not understood to be a place where the textual world of the Bible is to be inhabited, seminary leaders often ineffectively attempt to address this shortcoming by supplementing a student's curriculum with added life-oriented courses such as "spiritual formation."

While Sailhamer affirms the expressed goal of the "spiritual formation" efforts, he asserts the missing piece is the appreciation for a rightly-focused, text-community. He writes,

The aim and goal would be an intentional development in the seminary student of such qualities as Christian character and maturity, godly living, a strong marriage and family, as well as basic Bible knowledge and doctrine. The important point is not the subject matter of the courses but their goal, that is, developing the skills of working with the biblical text in context, specifically, the student's own context of the seminary community.

This text-community awareness will develop spiritual maturity through working with the biblical text with the community in mind. The skills for this type of biblical text work are developed through a particular approach to biblical hermeneutics, one that wants to see the textual meaning realized in the readers (or reading community). Reorienting students to their current living environment in addition to any future ministry plans allows for a collective focus on "practical skills in biblical hermeneutics which are directed at the student during the time he or she is a part of the seminary community itself."

In this way, close study of the biblical text informs a student's current thinking and pursuits as well as his or her future ministry of the Word. Likewise, faculty have an opportunity to refocus on and then emulate the values developed by the biblical authors themselves. The faculty fill a crucial role in teaching and holding to the "ideals and standards intended and taught by the authors of the biblical texts." When faculty members mentor students in this way, in other words, they serve as an embodied response to the meaning of the biblical writings.

This theological vision for seminary education repurposes the core activities of the seminary curriculum as the guidance of the Scriptures shapes the life of the community. The seminary that is also a text-community is necessarily a worshipping community that engages its current culture in accordance with the script of the biblical text. The disposition required for this vision is a high-view of Scripture's authority and a commitment to reading it with trained eyes and softened hearts. Accordingly, the seminary is the proper place for an academic study of the Scriptures, not simply because of its status as an academic community, but because of the seminary's status as a confessional text-community.

As this kind of textual community, the seminary is a qualitatively different academic setting than the university. In this intellectual and theological setting, interpreters study the meaning of biblical texts in light of core commitments to the authority and divinely inspired origin of these Scriptures. In this regard, Sailhamer argues that the seminary uniquely meets the "necessity of a sympathetic text-context for a proper exegesis of the Bible." For Sailhamer, the hermeneutical concept of a text-in-context and of a text's effective history complement this basic understanding of the theological educational institution. Because the seminary is situated within the larger domain of the Christian church (unlike the university), it is able to function as "a text-community shaped by the Bible within a context of an effective history that lies unbroken from the time of its composition."[8] In other words, the seminary, like the church, is a "living key to the Bible's meaning."

As such, the seminary is equipped in a unique way to apply the Scriptures to the needs of the church. The seminary is a community of faith that maintains the "congeniality" necessary for a proper understanding of the Bible. Sailhamer's contention at this point is that the seminary is thus "an instance of the Bible in context." Because the seminary is also embedded in the broader domain of the church, it also becomes a socially effective reality or "an instance of the Bible in culture." Serving as a realization of the Bible both *in context* and *in culture* allows the seminary to be "a test case for understanding texts in situations." In this way, the seminary becomes primarily a community of faith that wrestles with both the *meaning* and the *meaningfulness* of biblical texts. The element that connects the modern biblical reader to the textual intention of the ancient biblical author is the medium of the text and the affinity of faith.

Maintaining the focus and stability of the textual community will also allow a seminary to adapt to changing circumstances and address whatever new challenges may arise. As Sailhamer reflects, "Viewing the seminary as a textual community can also assist in the task of

---

8 Sailhamer demonstrates elsewhere his awareness of Hans-Georg Gadamer's work on effective history in *Wahrheit und Methode* (Mohr-Siebeck, 1975), but also the critique of Gadamer provided by E.D. Hirsch in *Validity in Interpretation* (Yale University Press, 1967). For example, see Sailhamer, *Introduction to Old Testament Theology: A Canonical Approach* (Zondervan, 1995), 93–96, 168–169, 218–220; and *Meaning of the Pentateuch: Revelation, Composition and Interpretation* (IVP, 2009), 68–98.

projecting goals and ideals for the seminary into the future. Simply put, whatever the future may hold, the central task of the seminary always remains the same—the interpretation of Scripture."

## The Strategic Significance of Biblical Hermeneutics

If a seminary is identified as a textual community, certain tasks that can serve multiple domains will naturally take priority. Moreover, in a *textual* community, the meaning of texts and the study of biblical hermeneutics serves a strategic and systemic function in the life and practice of the seminary. For Sailhamer, this interpretive task involves close attention to the compositional features of the canonical text within the context of a faith-filled textual community.

During the time that Sailhamer was preparing his address, he was also working on what would later be published as *Introduction to Old Testament Theology: A Canonical Approach*. In this extended study of biblical hermeneutics and the discipline of biblical theology, Sailhamer discusses further the notion of the effective history of texts and the nature of text-communities. For example in his discussion of a confessional hermeneutic, he observes that "the composition of the biblical books itself involved the hermeneutical task of interpreting authoritative texts. Thus the historical study of the composition of the OT cannot dispense with a consideration of its effective history."[9] Sailhamer also highlights the reciprocal relationship between biblical texts and the believing community that reads and receives these texts as authoritative Scripture. The communities of faith that produce and preserve biblical texts are also the same communities that are themselves produced and shaped by those texts.[10]

---

9 Sailhamer, *Introduction*, 180.

10 Sailhamer reflects further that "the same faith that lay behind the formation of the books of the OT was nourished, sustained, and propagated by those very books. The communities that ultimately were responsible for the preservation of the Hebrew Bible, Judaism, and Christianity, were themselves formed by the faith engendered in the Hebrew Bible" (*Introduction*, 180). In his study of the "Messiah and the Hebrew Bible," Sailhamer also draws upon this dynamic, noting that the "messianic thrust of the OT was the *whole* reason the books of the Hebrew Bible were written" ("Messiah and the Hebrew Bible," *JETS* 44.1 [March 2001]: 23). The Old Testament, in other words, was not written as the "national literature of Israel" or directly "to the

In his discussion of methodological choices an evangelical biblical theology must make, Sailhamer also considers the "sacred hermeneutic" (*hermeneutica sacra*) developed by Gerhard Maier.[11] Sailhamer sees Maier's sacred hermeneutic as a laudable example of a confessional approach to biblical theology that provides several insights into the relationship between a textual community and sound biblical interpretation. Foremost among these is that a biblical interpreter "must answer to the church" for "it is within that context that biblical interpretation must operate."[12] This type of confessional reading operates at an individual level as well as a corporate level. Sailhamer reflects, "it is only by placing ourselves under the authority of the biblical text and conforming our lives to it through prayer, repentance, godliness, that we can come to understand the meaning of the historical authors."[13]

Continuing to draw upon Maier's sacred hermeneutic (*hermeneutica sacra*), Sailhamer argues that biblical interpretation within a text-community must involve at least three basic steps. He explains first that "the biblical interpreter comes to the text as a continuation of his or her own situation in life, not as a distant object of study, but as the source for hearing God."[14] A confessional hermeneutic is a reading that recognizes the Bible as a direct divine address. The second element of this disposition involves recognizing that "in interpretation, one comes to the biblical text expecting a struggle between oneself and God who speaks in this text. The interpreter knows his or her own heart and its tendency to distort and change the voice of God which speaks in the text."[15] A confessional reading must involve repentance and a humble acknowledgment of the ways one might distort or

---

nation of Israel as such," but was likely written "as the expression of the deep-seated messianic hope of a small group of faithful prophets and their followers" (23). For a development of this notion that biblical texts generated the messianic hope in the believing community that preserved the Scriptures, see *Meaning of the Pentateuch*, 245–256; and "Biblical Theology and the Composition of the Hebrew Bible," in *Biblical Theology: Retrospect and Prospect*, ed. Scott J. Hafemann (IVP, 2002), 25–37.

11 See Gerhard Maier, *Biblical Hermeneutics*, trans. Robert W. Yarbrough (Crossway, 1994); and Sailhamer, *Introduction*, 234–237.

12 Sailhamer, *Introduction*, 235.

13 Sailhamer, *Introduction*, 235.

14 Sailhamer, *Introduction*, 236.

15 Sailhamer, *Introduction*, 236.

resist the meaning of biblical texts. Finally, Sailhamer concludes that a sacred hermeneutic encourages one to approach the Scripture with confidence while also "recognizing the deep dependency of the interpreter on a thorough familiarity with the meaning of the text itself. One strives to know it and expects a revelation, a basic insight, from it. One's position before Scripture must be characterized by prayerful expectation and humble openness."[16] The overall thrust of this discussion is that valid biblical interpretation should result in a changed biblical reader.

Due to its confessional approach, Sailhamer contends, the seminary text-community "is in a better position to understand the biblical text."[17] The meaning of the "biblical text is ongoing, not static" and the "original" meaning of the Scriptures "would include an intended response of the reader to the message proclaimed in the text."[18] The faithful Bible reader recognizes the authority of biblical literature and is a member of a textual community that is shaped by that authority. Faithful readers of the Scripture live the "quoted life" of the text as they interpret their daily life, their understanding of the way the world works, and the nature of their relationship with God through the lens of God's written revelation. In this way, we can meaningfully speak of biblical readers inhabiting the textual world of the Bible.

Sailhamer pursues the implications of these hermeneutical insights for theological education at key places in his address. He argues along these lines "that a crucial identity marker" for the seminary is "the relationship between the seminary and its embedded biblical text-world." A primary access to this text-world is through the analysis and proclamation of the biblical writings and the careful study of the original languages of those texts. However, the study of biblical literature is not aimed at "deriving static information from the biblical texts." On the contrary, Sailhamer contends that once the biblical text-world is accessed through careful reading, then that world must inform and engage the "life setting of the student." In *Introduction*, Sailhamer clarifies what he means by this "world" which is informed and shaped by the Scriptures. He writes, "The reader is invited to become a

---

16 Sailhamer, *Introduction*, 236.
17 Sailhamer, *Introduction*, 168.
18 Sailhamer, *Introduction*, 168.

part of that world and to make its history the framework for his or her own personal life. The reader of the Bible is called upon to submit to the reality represented in Scripture and to worship its Creator."[19]

The textual world of Scripture is not one merely fabricated by the biblical texts but instead is the reader's access to a true depiction of reality. Sailhamer reflects further that "the clear intent of the biblical narratives is to establish the fact that this is the only true account of the world."[20] When this reality is firmly in view, the reader has recognized the "true intent of the biblical narratives and the powerful influence these narratives were, and are, capable of exerting on society and the life of the individual."[21] As a faith-filled reader of Scripture within a textual community, a seminary student's thoughts, habits, relationships, and daily pursuits can all be transformed and made meaningful. In his address, Sailhamer recognizes that the connection between Scripture and daily life is not artificial due to the comprehensive nature of a textual community. As he observes, the "corollary concepts of 'effective history' and 'quoted life' discussed above, provide a genuine link to the application of scriptural texts to life settings."

Sailhamer considers some of the practical and pedagogical implications of this framework in the second half of his address. As he evaluates several curriculum models for seminaries, he maintains a focus on the strategic significance of biblical hermeneutics in a textual community. He thus returns at several points to consider the function of the biblical languages in a seminary curriculum. To accomplish this, he establishes two key starting points.

First, he recognizes that the biblical text and the world it produces is discerned primarily through study of the biblical languages and secondarily through translations. Sailhamer's comments do not derive from language snobbery but something much more fundamental to his address, namely, "the textual nature of the seminary and the Christian church." He explains that "the subtleties of the use of a language in texts and the communities generated by them is such that

---

19 Sailhamer, *Introduction*, 216.
20 Sailhamer, *Introduction*, 217.
21 Sailhamer, *Introduction*, 217. See also Sailhamer's development of the notion of the "world of the text" and "cosmic map" in chapter six below ("The Eclipse of Old Testament Narrative").

[an exclusive use of only supplementary tools] in a foreign language is not likely to help grasp its meaning in texts." Rather, a working knowledge and basic competency in the original languages is necessary to equip students to observe the meaning of biblical texts and the effect of textual strategies that are seen best by close reading of Old Testament Hebrew and New Testament Greek.

Second, Sailhamer argues that the biblical languages give the student access to the most robust material for the areas of study that he characterizes as "Tasks 1" (Exegesis, Doctrine, Devotion), which then become the basis for the practices involved in "Tasks 2" (Homiletics, Christian Education, Pastoral Ministry) and "Tasks 3" (Missions/ Evangelism, Theology, Ethics). If biblical languages are not taught to all students in the seminary then the logistical result is a multiplication of seminary offerings (language-based and non-language based) throughout all three levels of the "Tasks." This multiplication can often lead to the isolation of students from one another as they pursue different coursework and also develop differing conceptions of the tasks of Christian ministry. Moreover, disciplines like systematic theology, preaching, and missions must function in this scenario with a more restricted access to the biblical text.

Because greater access to textual meaning is granted through the biblical languages, this study of the biblical languages serves the "tasks" in all domains, not just those in the category of Tasks 1. Furthermore, the pursuits of Tasks 1 are not more important than Tasks 2 and Tasks 3. Rather, the areas of study characterized as Tasks 1 are foundational for the other two sets of tasks due to the "domains" in which they operate.

*Further Implications of the Vision for Seminary Curricula*

With Sailhamer's vision of the seminary as a textual community and the needed interpretative tools to facilitate such a vision, there are several further implications of his address for a seminary's overall purpose and its curriculum. Four areas are addressed by Sailhamer as he considers the seminary's internal structure and its external relationships and as he looks to the seminary's present responsibilities and its future challenges. These implications also serve as a touchpoint to some of the ongoing discussions about the nature of the seminary that have continued in the decades since this address.

First, a seminary text-community implies a focused relationship between the disciplines. Being committed to this relationship means that seminary leaders must be committed "to 'reading' the text and 'steering' the community" according to it. For leadership to steer the seminary community with consistency and competence, the task of "locating" the community (i.e. its relationship to the church and the world) is a continual one. Practical pressures might cause well-meaning seminary leaders to shift focus from the text-community's integrated tasks, namely, reading the biblical text in life situations. Sailhamer questions the presupposition of an "alleged dichotomy between the practical and theoretical departments" because "a textually defined *theologia* means that at a fundamental level, every aspect of a seminary curriculum involves a similar task, that is, the interpretation (*traditio*) of Scripture (*traditum*)." Sailhamer recognizes that "surface tensions will inevitably continue to exist between departments in a seminary because there will always be wide divergences in specific contexts of application." Despite this understandable inter-disciplinary dynamic, Sailhamer concludes that a unified purpose is worth pursuing because fundamentally "all departments within a seminary must fulfill the same task, the application of Scripture to life."

Second, a seminary text-community requires a purposeful structural relationship between faculty and curriculum. The paired impulses of reading and locating also call for a multi-disciplinary faculty who can work across disciplines ("trans-disciplinary") to accomplish these ends. Sailhamer calls for the various disciplines to be driven by the interpretation of Scripture, which then creates "a pervasive unity of purpose within a textual community such as a seminary in that each member is entrusted with the same theoretical problems—meaning in texts." This textual impulse not only affects the "applied disciplines" such as evangelism, homiletics, or counseling, but it also shapes the way we view the core disciplines of biblical and theological studies. As Sailhamer reflects, "In a seminary conceived of as a textual community, every aspect of the curriculum, e.g., Hebrew Exegesis, is also seen as practical, that is, an application of the text to a life situation. . . . What exegesis is forced to face in a textual community is that the texts and its meaning have, in actual fact, already played a major role in shaping the life setting to which it is being applied. That setting is the Christian church."

The end result for faculty in this seminary vision is that each member must be committed to interpreting biblical texts within their given tasks (i.e. academic fields). The final shape of the curriculum is where "reading" and "locating" occur throughout a student's progress in an academic program. Shared faculty vision for this hermeneutical approach increases the ability of a seminary to foster a fully-orbed text-community that features an organic integration of this textual vision into each course regardless of its location among the academic disciplines.

Third, perceiving the seminary as a text-community has significant implications for the appropriate relationship between the academy and the church. Here the twin tasks of reading (the text) and locating (the community) must receive equal attention. Faculty and students engage and produce scholarship in this community with varied goals and specific audiences. Academic endeavors provide the tools for the sound reading of texts. Textual features and compositional shape guide interpretation as advanced skills are applied. Alongside these academic activities, students are also driven to read and embody textual meaning among their peers as they pursue gospel-centered relationships in view of their studies and ministry of the Word.

Moreover, in this model faculty members develop their expertise in ways that enhance the ability of the seminary community to study and embody biblical texts with excellence. Academic pursuits driven by questions more fitting to a university (not a biblical text-community) may perhaps be present but would not dominate seminary scholarship. Sailhamer contends that the expectation of "scholarship" in the seminary must be of the same quality in both reading and locating. He explains, "That is, the 'reading' of the text should be done with the same level of expertise as that of 'locating' the community." Scholarship in a textual community, in other words, will develop *tools for reading* (hermeneutics, original languages, text theory, various criticisms such as textual criticism, canonical criticism, text linguistics and compositional criticism) alongside of *tools for locating* (cultural criticism, phenomenology, linguistics, apologetics, systematic theology). These academic endeavors are pursued in tandem because the "ability to work with the original biblical language is as essential as sensitivity to culture."

Finally, understanding the seminary as a text-community allows for flexibility in theological education as it seeks to envision its agenda and face future challenges. In his discussion of the logistics of residential theological education, Sailhamer recognizes that the seminary landscape is changing in terms of how "community" is formed and maintained as new educational delivery systems are developed. In the twenty-five years since his address was given, much has changed in American and global cultures. However, the enduring value of conceiving of a seminary as a textual community is that this orientation on the study and effect of biblical texts can remain central even as modes of delivery, societal norms, and cultural pressures shift.

Though technology advances will always open new possibilities for content delivery and pedagogical adaptation, these advances also give the opportunity to extend the text-community beyond where previous generations of seminaries could consider. Integration with undergraduate programs (at a distance or nearby) and global text-communities are current possibilities worth pursuing. As outside forces require schools to find creative ways to continue their work and maintain their mission (as a result of either practical pressures, politics, or pandemics!), a clearly defined and coherent vision for a theological seminary is an increasingly valuable and necessary asset.

## Shared Concerns: Dialogue Partners in an Ongoing Conversation

One further way of seeing the enduring value of Sailhamer's vision for theological education is to consider some dialogue partners with a shared set of concerns in the ongoing conversation about theological education. The plan for a theological seminary that Sailhamer develops in his address resonates with other proposals that seek to shape the tasks of theological education in light of a controlling set of textual and theological parameters.

## The Textual Community and the Culture of Theology

As noted above, the notion of the seminary as a "textual community" is significant for Sailhamer's understanding of the educational task. A helpful complement to this conception is the way theologian John Webster envisions the task of theological education in terms of a "culture of theology."[22] Webster defines a Christian culture broadly as "the assembly of forms and practices which seeks somehow to inhabit the world which is brought into being by the staggering good news of Jesus Christ, the world of the new creation."[23] In Webster's approach, the work of theology "flourishes best when it has deep roots in the region, the cultural space, which is constituted by Christian faith and its confession of the gospel."[24]

What is required, then, is a "theological ethnography" which consists of a "theological depiction of the world of the church in which theology happens."[25] Within this ecclesial context, the pressing task is to develop "textual practices" or "habits of reading." As Webster urges, few things are "more necessary for the renewal of Christian theology than the promotion of awed reading of classical Christian texts." The traditions of "paraphrase and commentary" are the means by which the culture of theology is sustained. Those who train in this way have the simple yet challenging goal of becoming "a certain kind of person, one shaped by the culture of Christian faith."[26]

---

22 See John Webster, *The Culture of Theology*, ed. Ivor J. Davison and Alden McCray (Baker, 2019).

23 Webster, *Culture of Theology*, 43. He further elaborates that a culture is "a space or region made up of human activities" and a "set of intentional patterns of human action which have sufficient coherence, scope, and duration to constitute a way of life" (48).

24 Webster, *Culture of Theology*, 44. As he notes, "What inhibits Christian theology is not only the generally inhospitable intellectual and institutional environment in which it has to flourish but its lack of roots in the traditions of Christian belief and practice which are the soil in which it can grow" (44).

25 Webster, *Culture of Theology*, 45.

26 Webster, *Culture of Theology*, 45. Webster also recognizes the overlapping domains of the church and the world: "The theologian will thus not only be a skilled inhabitant of a particular cultural world but will demonstrate skills in reaching judgments about circumstance, and skills in reading his or her situation well" (59).

This theological orientation of a confessional approach to the culture of theology requires a re-thinking of the curricular shape of theological education. As Webster notes, "taking a different direction here will mean a reevaluation of the kinds of competencies which are thought indispensable for undertaking the task of Christian theology."[27] The controlling center of this theological reorientation involves the effect of an authoritative text. "One of the main tasks of theology," Webster explains, "is to exemplify and promote close and delighted reading of Holy Scripture as the *viva vox Dei*, the voice of the risen Jesus to his community."[28] Consequently, the "rhetoric of theology" is to be "largely governed by proximity and subordination to the text of Scripture as the place where the gospel is laid bare."[29] Moreover, the occupation of the theologian is "primarily exegetical" and thus "concern with other business is only derivative or by extension."[30]

Even within the academy, the task of theology must maintain its focus on its own distinctive ends. As Webster asserts, "There is never a point at which Christian theology can absolve itself from the task of articulating its own world."[31] Because of its dependence on the Scriptures, "the tasks of exegesis and dogmatics are never finished, even temporarily."[32] This theological and textual orientation marks the distinctive contribution that the discipline of theology makes to the broader academy.[33]

---

27  Webster, *Culture of Theology*, 57.
28  Webster, *Culture of Theology*, 64.
29  Webster, *Culture of Theology*, 65.
30  Webster, *Culture of Theology*, 65. Webster recognizes here too that this orientation requires a robust theology of the Scriptures and a Spirit-guided reading of the Bible.
31  Webster, *Culture of Theology*, 113.
32  Webster, *Culture of Theology*, 113.
33  Webster notes to this effect that when exegesis and dogmatics "cease to be matters of present activity and become simply an inheritance hovering in the background, then all too quickly Christian theology falls into the kind of confused or incoherent grasp of its proper subject matter, which not only weakens Christian identity but also robs it of anything pungent to say in the wider academy" (113). "As a rule," he concludes, "the more confident theology is in its own native habits of thought and speech, the more savory will be its contribution to the world of higher learning" (113). Webster also provides an extended reflection on the curricular structure of theological training within a "culture of theology" in *Holy Scripture: A Dogmatic Sketch* (Cambridge, 2003), 107–135; "God, Theology, Universities," in *God Without*

## The World of the Text and the Drama of Doctrine

In his development of the seminary as a textual community, Sailhamer also notes the interpretive significance of the "world of the text" and the formative role it plays for a people of the book. In certain ways, Kevin Vanhoozer echoes Sailhamer and Webster's concerns as he articulates the task of theology in light of an orienting focus drawn from the grand storyline of the biblical canon. Vanhoozer develops the notion of redemptive history as a "theodrama" in which God speaks and acts on behalf of his people.[34] In this theodrama, individual believers have a "speaking part" which centers on understanding and proclaiming "what is in Christ."[35] Accordingly, a theologian is one who has studied the script of the theodrama and helps pastors and believers recognize and enact their divinely commissioned roles in local churches and communities.

This broad framework draws together central insights about the shape of the grand storyline of the Bible, the vocation of theologians, and the nature of discipleship among the churches. Theologians, then, require by necessity a working knowledge of the whole of Scripture, theology, and pastoral ministry. To participate in this kind of ministry among the churches requires pastor-theologians who are able to harness the tools of the entire spectrum of theological disciplines.

This understanding of the role of doctrine in the life of the churches also entails a recognition of the importance of the comprehensive view of the world generated by the Scriptures. If the scope of the theodrama encompasses all of life, then the Christian theologian must be skilled at understanding and embracing the world of the biblical text and also be able to discern and critically engage the "social

---

*Measure: Working Papers in Christian Theology*, Vol. 2 (T&T Clark, 2018), 157–172; and "Theological Theology," in *T&T Clark Reader in John Webster*, ed. Michael Allen (T&T Clark, 2020), 21–42.

34 For an entryway into Vanhoozer's controlling thesis in this regard, see Kevin J. Vanhoozer, *The Drama of Doctrine: A Canonical-Linguistic Approach to Christian Theology* (WJK, 2005), 1–33.

35 See especially Kevin J. Vanhoozer, *Faith Speaking Understanding: Performing the Drama of Doctrine* (WJK, 2014), 1–47; and *Pictures at a Theological Exhibition: Scenes of the Church's Worship, Witness and Wisdom* (IVP, 2016).

imaginaries" that hold sway in contemporary contexts.³⁶ Part of the focus of theological education should therefore include doctrine and theological interpretation, and also discipleship and cultural analysis. In other words, the path of a pastor-theologian involves being and equipping others to be both *hearers* and *doers*.³⁷

*Biblical Theology and the Shape of a Curriculum*

When discussing the implementation of this vision of training in biblical and theological studies, these thinkers seek to cast a vision that centers on theological and literary features of the proper object and subject of study: The living God revealed in the Scriptures. A complementary focus is pursued by biblical theologian Graeme Goldsworthy in his writing and academic leadership at Moore Theological College. Once he became convinced of the need for a biblical theology that sought to articulate the message of the whole Bible on its own terms, Goldsworthy began working to integrate this type of study into his teaching and training of ministers in Australia.³⁸ For our purpose here, Goldsworthy explains that because biblical theology seeks to capture the scope and shape of biblical revelation, it must also hold a central place in the explicit and implicit curriculum of the seminary. From the one-year diploma for lay persons to the

---

36 See Kevin J. Vanhoozer, *Hearers & Doers: A Pastor's Guide to Making Disciples Through Scripture and Doctrine* (Lexham, 2019), 1–42. In dialogue with the work of Charles Taylor, Vanhoozer develops the notion of "social imaginary" as "the picture that frames our everyday beliefs and practices" and the "nest of background assumptions, often implicit, that lead people to feel things as right or wrong, correct or incorrect" (8). A social imaginary is like a "root metaphor" that shapes a person's "perception of the world, undergirds one's worldview, and funds one's plausibility structures" (8–9).

37 Vanhoozer, *Hearers & Doers*, 43–87. Vanhoozer succinctly applies these starting points to the task of theological education in "How Theologians are Relearning How to Read the Bible as Scripture," in *Didaktikos* (February 2020): 34–35. Cf. also Daniel J. Treier, *Virtue and the Voice of God: Toward Theology as Wisdom* (Eerdmans, 2006). Treier develops and extends the vision articulated by Vanhoozer in the realm of theological education, emphasizing the controlling aim of practical wisdom (*phronesis*) in theological studies.

38 See Goldsworthy's account of this development in "Biblical Theology in the Seminary and Bible College," in *SBJT* 12.4 (Winter 2008): 20–35; and *Christ-Centered Biblical Theology: Hermeneutical Foundations and Principles* (IVP, 2012), 19–37, 76–99.

advanced PhD degree, a strategic course of biblical theology should be made a requirement. This move is designed to improve biblical literacy but also to integrate the various elements of a given degree program.[39]

Part of Goldsworthy's emphasis on biblical theology follows from his conviction that the gospel message should be a central and structuring element of Christian ministry and study of the Scriptures. With this orienting center, the disciplines would be distinct but unified as they each play their discrete part in explicating and communicating the gospel. As part of the explicit curriculum, courses on biblical theology formally make connections between the disciplines. As part of the implicit curriculum of a school, individual biblical scholars and theologians would teach their subject matter with an eye toward how their discipline informs and is influenced by the focus on redemptive history that culminates in the gospel of Jesus Christ.[40]

Moreover, "because Christian ministry is gospel ministry, seminary teachers need to understand that we are all *inter*-dependent in our own specialties. Our common love of the Bible means that we should be more aware of how the Bible is being taught and applied in courses other than our own."[41] Because of the gospel focus of a confessional seminary, Goldsworthy concludes that an "evangelical institution is in an overall better position to shape a biblically based course than an institution driven by liberalism."[42] Accordingly, Goldsworthy's perennial encouragement to educators is for "every seminary and Bible college [to] take up the challenge to provide an introductory course in

---

[39] Goldsworthy, "Biblical Theology in the Seminary," 24. This curricular decision made biblical theology above all others a "distinct and compulsory course" for every student at Moore Theological College (24). As Goldsworthy notes, without a biblical theology course, "there was nothing to require any interaction between the subjects" (24). He also expresses that particularly concerning was "the fact that the current academic ethos encouraged the complete separation of the two parts of biblical studies: Old Testament and New Testament" (24).

[40] Goldsworthy summarizes that "the explicit curriculum" is "what the school intentionally and in reality offers to students" and the "implied curriculum" is the "non-salient aspects of what the school in fact teaches students but not intentionally" (30). For Goldsworthy, the study of biblical theology should be anchored in a seminary's explicit curriculum and also embodied in the implied curriculum as well.

[41] Goldsworthy, "Biblical Theology in the Seminary," 32.

[42] Goldsworthy, "Biblical Theology in the Seminary," 29.

'big picture' biblical theology and then strive to keep the vision alive in the way biblical studies are conducted."[43]

## Theological Training and the Life of the Churches

A common thread in these models and proposals is a close connection between theological training and the life of the churches. For evangelical theological education, there is a pressing need to demonstrate an organic link between the academy and the churches at both a formal and informal level. For example, pastor-theologian John Piper articulates a vision for theological education that is directly related to the context of the churches. As he states, "We cannot overemphasize the importance of our seminaries in shaping the theology and spirit of the churches and denominations and missionary enterprise," for the "tone of the classrooms and teachers exerts profound effect on the tone of our pulpits."[44] For Piper, what is needed is both a "pastoral theology" and a "philosophy of theological education."[45]

With the development of Bethlehem College and Seminary in Minneapolis, Minnesota, Piper has sought to implement a vision for theological education that locates the academy squarely within the church by means of a clear theological foundation that shapes pedagogical practice, namely, God's glory and the satisfaction of believers in the God of the gospel.[46] Accordingly, the goal of theological

---

43 Goldsworthy, "Biblical Theology in the Seminary," 32. He also adds that it is "doubly important that evangelical colleges teach biblical theology, deliberately, intentionally, and not just hope that the biblical studies teachers between them will get the message across" (32).

44 John Piper, "Brothers, Pray for the Seminary!" (January 1, 1995): https://www.desiringgod.org/articles/brothers-pray-for-the-seminary.

45 On the logistics of this dynamic between pastoral theology and theological education, see too John Piper and D. A. Carson, *The Pastor as Scholar & The Scholar as Pastor: Reflections on Life and Ministry* (Crossway, 2011); and Todd Wilson and Gerald L. Hiestand, eds., *Becoming a Pastor-Theologian: New Possibilities for Church Leadership* (IVP, 2016).

46 Piper articulates the beginnings and development of his school in "The Greatest Things Have Not Changed: Bethlehem College & Seminary Ten Years Later" (November 5, 2018): https://www.desiringgod.org/articles/brothers-pray-for-the-seminary. He summarizes this connection by noting that "since we aim in our education to glorify God in all we think and do, and since he is not glorified as he ought to

education is to inform minds with biblical and theological truth but through the process of shaping lives for Christian ministry.

As Piper emphasizes, the aim is "to build into the student habits of mind and heart that will never leave them and will fit them for a lifetime of ongoing growth. The well-educated person is the person who has the habits of mind and heart to go on learning what he needs to learn to live in a Christ-exalting way for the rest of his life – and that would apply to whatever sphere of life he pursues."[47] Piper's approach to theological education, then, resonates with Sailhamer's contention that "though it has links to numerous other institutions (e.g., Academia), the seminary, as such, exists *because of* and *in behalf* of the Christian church."[48]

These contemporary dialogue partners help illustrate some of the central components of Sailhamer's vision for theological education and also help highlight the unique aspects of his approach to the shape of a seminary. More examples could be explored both from recent approaches and also models for theological education that have been established and developed throughout the history of the churches.

For example, drawing on examples from the early church and medieval era, Lewis Ayres articulates the urgent necessity for the shape of historical and theological education to follow directly from "first principles."[49] Similarly, Robert Kolb examines Martin Luther's priorities

---

be in hearts where he is not treasured above all things, therefore, it is essential that we instill in students the unabashed, unwavering habit of pursuing more satisfaction in God than in any other treasure in the world."

47 John Piper, "The Earth is the Lord's: The Supremacy of Christ in Christian Learning" (November 5, 2008): https://www.desiringgod.org/messages/the-earth-is-the-lords-the-supremacy-of-christ-in-christian-learning. Cf. Piper's "qualified enthusiasm for higher learning" in *Think: The Life of the Mind and the Love of God* (Crossway, 2010), 167–175.

48 Moreover, Bethlehem College & Seminary also serves as an example and a development of the situation Sailhamer mentions in the second part of his address, namely, a smaller seminary located within the domain of a larger local church. In his reflection on Sailhamer's life and scholarship, Piper mentions some of their extensive exchanges about biblical interpretation and the nature of theological education. See "For the Name and Word of God: My Tribute to John Sailhamer (1946–2017)," https://www.desiringgod.org/articles/for-the-name-and-word-of-god.

49 See Lewis Ayres, "On the Practice and Teaching of Christian Doctrine," *Gregorianum* 80.1 (1999): 33-94. Ayres begins his lengthy discussion of the practices and virtues that attend the teaching of Christian doctrine with a close reading of the

in general and theological education and how those starting points shaped the academic community at Wittenberg in the Reformation era.[50] Moreover, Paul House commends Dietrich Bonhoeffer's model of seminary training that emphasized the critical importance of "life together" for Christian ministry even at great cost.[51] Highlighting the need for careful consideration of inter-disciplinary concerns and in dialogue with the current field of hermeneutics, Craig Bartholomew also speaks of an "ecology of Christian scholarship" within which theological education relates to academic work in other disciplines.[52] Aspects of these historical and contemporary approaches help situate Sailhamer's vision for a theological seminary that is relentlessly focused on the Scriptures, maintains a clear connection to academic scholarship, and is oriented to the life of the churches.

## Closing Reflection

For theological educators who are seeking to uphold an evangelical theology of the Scriptures and also prepare students for ministry in dialogue with the highest level of academic rigor, Sailhamer's understanding of the nature, purpose, and tasks of a seminary remains encouraging and instructive. Encouraging because it represents a compelling vision of the organic integration of careful study of Scripture

---

opening of Thomas Aquinas's *Summa Theologiae* and Gregory of Nazianzus's *Theological Orations*.

50 See Robert Kolb, *Martin Luther and the Enduring Word of God: The Wittenberg School and Its Scripture-Centered Proclamation* (Baker, 2016); and William M. Marsh, "Martin Luther: Education for the Preservation of the Gospel and Society," in *A Legacy of Religious Educators*, ed. E. L. Towns and B. K. Forrest (Liberty, 2016), 109–135.

51 Paul House, *Bonhoeffer's Seminary Vision: A Case for Costly Discipleship and Life Together* (Crossway, 2015). House argues that Bonhoeffer "left a legacy of determined commitment to incarnational seminary education" (184). House explains that "his vision of theological education was not simply informational or formational. It was both. He did not believe in giving up academic or formational rigor. His desire to build more faithful churches was inextricably linked to his view of the personal shaping of pastors" (184).

52 See Craig G. Bartholomew, "Scripture and the University: The Ecology of Christian Scholarship," in *Introducing Biblical Hermeneutics: A Comprehensive Framework for Hearing God in Scripture* (Baker, 2015), 463–484. In this vein, compare the range of reflective essays in *The Bible and the University*, ed. David Lyle Jeffrey and C. Stephen Evans (Zondervan, 2007).

and faithful ministry among the churches. Instructive because the task of envisioning and articulating a coherent seminary curriculum is still an ever-present responsibility of those involved in the academic study of the Bible in every generation.

# Part 2:
# Hermeneutics, History, and Disciplinary Dialogue

# 3

# Hermeneutics, History, and Disciplinary Dialogue in Sailhamer's Scholarship

## By Ched Spellman

IN PART 2, WE INCLUDE SEVERAL of Sailhamer's articles, essays, and reviews that are less well-known yet relate to some of the major topics he develops in his address on theological education. In his address, Sailhamer argues that because theological training centers on the written texts of Scripture, "the nature and task of a Christian seminary is fundamentally hermeneutical." As Sailhamer engages various disciplines throughout his career, he maintains a focus on the textual nature of biblical writings and the hermeneutical implications of this reality.[1]

One of Sailhamer's consistent contributions to the ongoing dialogue in evangelical scholarship has a complementary focus: Have we adequately reckoned with the fact that God has revealed himself through written texts? In one sense, Sailhamer's entire scholarly project could be characterized as the working out of this prevailing hermeneutical concern. With this focus, Sailhamer's body of work is distinctive but not idiosyncratic, as this specific concern addresses a central feature of biblical interpretation and an evangelical theology of Scripture. As Stephen Chapman keenly observes, "No one in

---

1 An initial example of the way Sailhamer engages various disciplines is the series of introductory volumes he published in the Zondervan Quick Reference Series (Zondervan, 1998). These books include studies on biblical archaeology, biblical prophecy, biblical survey, Christian theology, canon formation, the life of Christ, and Old Testament history. His full-Bible commentary also shows a facility in both testaments as well as a desire to communicate to pastors and biblical readers on a popular level. See *NIV Compact Bible Commentary* (Zondervan, 1994).

evangelical scholarship perceived as early or as perceptively as John Sailhamer how increased awareness of the biblical canon might helpfully reorient evangelical hermeneutics, especially in thinking about history."[2]

An example of this broad engagement and focused concern can be seen in a brief article Sailhamer wrote in *Christianity Today* entitled, "What have they done to my Genesis?"[3] In the mid-90s, talk-show host Bill Moyers led a series of discussions on PBS called *Genesis: A Living Conversation* in which a group of various authors, clergy, and scholars from diverse religious backgrounds discussed the Genesis narratives. This group read the stories at face value and grappled with what they found there. Why, they wondered, did Abel die a brutal death although he obeyed God, and why did Cain get to build the first city although he was a murderer? This fact seemed much more troubling to some than Cain's actual act of murder. What hope is there for those who live in Abel-like obedience? What do you do with a story like this?

Reflecting on watching this discussion, Sailhamer observes:

> As I watched it, it occurred to me that, as evangelicals, the Bible may be our Cinderella. We have opened our homes to her, but we have relegated her to washing our dishes and scrubbing our floors. We have used her to make our lives theologically comfortable; and she, never one to complain, has remained faithful. But we have been blind to her true loveliness and oblivious to the possibility that others might see real beauty in her. As the series clearly showed, our Cinderella has been to the ball, and the glass slipper has been found. The king's men are now knocking at our door, searching for the beauty they have seen in "our" Scriptures.

---

2 Stephen B. Chapman, "Reclaiming Inspiration for the Bible," in *Canon and Biblical Interpretation*, ed. Craig G. Bartholomew, et al., Scripture and Hermeneutics Series 7 (Zondervan, 2006), 182. Chapman critically interacts with Sailhamer's position but also highlights the significance of his overall approach to biblical texts.

3 See John Sailhamer, "What Have They Done to My Genesis? To my surprise, the PBS series showed me how I'd underestimated Scripture," in *Christianity Today* (January 6, 1997), 46–47.

Sailhamer then considers the fact that these casual readers were taking the stories seriously and attempting to discern how these jarring accounts affect our reality. He wonders why evangelicals are sometimes not the ones to produce such a serious, penetrating look at the book of Genesis on its own terms:

> The answer in part, I believe, is that we evangelicals have become adept at defending the Bible from its adversaries; we have produced a formidable and effective body of literature supporting our case. In the process, however, we have forgotten to ask seriously what it all means. Perhaps we mistakenly assumed that because no one was interested in the stories of the Bible, the stories themselves were uninteresting.

He concludes his reflection by urging, "We must look our Cinderella in the face and see her beauty. We must be willing to take her on her own terms—to live in her world, to see our lives as part of her world, and to seek to live according to it. We must not call on her solely to do the menial, and often demeaning, tasks of making our lives apologetically comfortable."

In his first published article at the beginning of his academic career, Sailhamer articulates this same set of emphases. In a discussion about the textual features of Genesis 1-11, Sailhamer aims "to explore in a general way the broader question of the meaning of biblical narrative texts. How do we go about finding what the biblical writers were teaching in their carefully wrought narratives?"[4] In reading biblical narrative, "one must not only look at the course of the event in its historical setting but one must also look for the purpose and intention of the author in recounting the event."[5] Highlighting the significance of this hermeneutical insight, Sailhamer summarizes his approach by connecting it with the theological presuppositions of an evangelical view of the Scriptures:

---

4 John Sailhamer, "Exegetical Notes: Genesis 1:1–2:4a," *Trinity Journal* 5.1 (Spring 1984): 74.

5 Sailhamer, "Exegetical Notes: Genesis 1:1–2:4a," 74.

The ideas of looking beyond the historical event to the author's version of it does not imply that the author's version is different than the event as it actually happened. Rather, in historical narrative what is given is the inspired author's evaluation of the meaning and significance of the event. In historical narrative we may be told less than all that happened, but we are also told much more than simply that the event happened—although we are always being told at least that. We are also being told the purpose and significance of the event within the broader context of God's revelation in his word.[6]

In his subsequent works, Sailhamer continues to hone these instincts about the nature of narrative, the portrayal of historical events, a high view of Scripture as revelation, and the messianic heartbeat of biblical theology. In his biblical-theological commentary on the Pentateuch, Sailhamer interprets Genesis through Deuteronomy as a compositional whole and with an eye toward the interpretive nature of narrative.[7] In his introduction to the field of Old Testament studies and biblical theology, he further articulates the crucial significance of the hermeneutical choice of "Text or Event" when reading the narratives of the Bible.[8]

When Sailhamer joined the faculty at Southeastern Baptist Theological Seminary in 1999, he summed up his scholarly work and

---

6 Sailhamer, "Exegetical Notes: Genesis 1:1–2:4a," 74.

7 See John Sailhamer, *Pentateuch as Narrative: A Biblical-Theological Commentary* (Zondervan, 1992). Sailhamer notes here that the simple fact that biblical texts have inspired biblical authors "makes a text-oriented approach to exegesis and biblical theology crucial for the evangelical" (22). Further, "our task is not to explain what happened to Israel in OT times. Though worthy of our efforts, archaeology and history must not be confused with exegesis and biblical theology. We must recognize that the authors of Scripture have already made it their task to tell us in their texts what happened to Israel. The task that remains for us is to explain and proclaim what they have written" (22).

8 See John Sailhamer, *Introduction to Old Testament Theology: A Canonical Approach* (Zondervan, 1995), 36–85. In this extended discussion, Sailhamer explains that "the issue we are attempting to raise here is simply that of our commitment to an inspired *written* Word of God as the locus of God's special revelation. For the Christian today we must again raise the question: Where does the locus of God's special revelation lie? Does it lie in the meaning of historical events provided by the Scriptures or does it lie in the meaning we ourselves attach to the events of Israel's history?" (42).

emphasis in the classroom by stating, "The Old Testament is saying the same thing everywhere you look.... The identity of Christ as the Messiah promised beforehand in the Hebrew Scriptures is central to the gospel."[9] After being elected president of the Evangelical Theological Society in the following year, he chose as his topic, "The Messiah and the Hebrew Bible."[10] He concludes that "the books of the OT were written as the embodiment of a real, messianic hope—a hope in a future miraculous work of God in sending a promised Redeemer."[11]

Moreover, in his final published work, *The Meaning of the Pentateuch*, Sailhamer continues to sound this clarion call to think carefully about the nature of biblical narrative and the textual strategies of biblical authors.[12] In an interview about the book, Sailhamer articulates again this scholarly focus that he maintains and develops over his thirty-year career.[13] When asked to explain the meaning of the Pentateuch "to evangelicals who revere these foundational books but do not see their relevance," Sailhamer responds in this way:

> Experience has taught me that we really have to want to understand the meaning of the Pentateuch before we see its relevance for our lives. I've been fortunate to have students who have kept me looking for answers about the meaning and relevance of this book. The old theologians used to speak of "the love for Scripture"

---

9 See "Renowned Hebrew scholar to join Southeastern Seminary's faculty," *Baptist Press* (April 19, 1999). During this transition, Sailhamer also notes the underlying motivation for his focus on the original biblical languages: "You can read the Bible in any translation, but there is something about evangelicals taking seriously the fact that these are the inspired words of God" ("5 new professors join Southeastern faculty," *Baptist Press*, August 20, 1999).

10 See John Sailhamer, "The Messiah and the Hebrew Bible," *JETS* 44.1 (March 2001): 5–23.

11 Sailhamer, "The Messiah and the Hebrew Bible," 23.

12 See John Sailhamer, *The Meaning of the Pentateuch: Revelation, Composition and Interpretation* (IVP, 2009). He notes in the introduction that he "follows an approach that looks for the biblical author's 'intention' in the 'verbal meaning' of his book. It seeks the meaning of his words, phrases and sentences. How do the individual pieces fit together within the whole? Central to the aim of this book is the discovery of the compositional strategy of the biblical author of the Pentateuch" (11).

13 See "Finding Meaning in the Pentateuch: Powerful Endorsements bolster John Sailhamer's new tome on the Bible's first five books," interview by Collin Hansen in *Christianity Today* (January 11, 2010).

as a sign of true faith in Christ. They would say, "We should read the Old Testament as if it were written with the blood of Christ." For them, the Old Testament and the Pentateuch in particular was a Christian book, a book about Christ. For most evangelical Christians today it is a book about archaeology and ancient history.

Here we have to be careful because, to be sure, the Old Testament is about ancient history. But that is not its meaning. Its meaning is Christ. Saying that also calls for a great deal of caution. In my book, I take the view that the whole of the Pentateuch is about Christ, but that doesn't mean that Christ is in the whole Pentateuch. Finding Christ in the Pentateuch means learning to see him when he is there rather than trying to see him when he is not there. I like to tell my students that we don't need to spiritualize the Old Testament to find Christ, but we do need to read it with spiritual eyes.

I have a good friend who likes to chide me by saying you don't need "exegesis" to find Christ in the Old Testament. All we need is some "extra Jesus." I wrote my book in part to show my friend and others like him that serious scholarship leads one to find Christ in the Old Testament because he is really there. The author of the Pentateuch put him there when he wrote the book. I've found that if you show someone that Christ is really there in the Pentateuch and the Old Testament, they will come back to "see more," not merely because they have come to revere the Pentateuch as a foundational book, but more importantly because they want to see more of Jesus.

He concludes the interview by answering a question about what he thought the "next great frontier" in Old Testament studies would be. In the final published words of his academic career, Sailhamer echoes an emphasis that runs like a nerve center throughout his body of work. "The next frontier in Old Testament studies," he insists, "will be the same as its first frontier, that is, the question of the Old Testament's witness to Christ."

The following essays in this volume represent some of Sailhamer's interaction with the broader field of biblical studies from the vantage point of his hermeneutical approach to exegesis and biblical theology.

In them, Sailhamer discusses the study of Hebrew grammar ("Reading the Bible as a Text"), the relevance of biblical archaeology ("Archaeology and the Reliability of the Old Testament"), the nature of biblical narrative ("Eclipse of Old Testament Narrative"), the use of historical background information in exegesis ("Role of History in Biblical Interpretation"), and scholarly works in biblical studies and systematic theology ("Selected Book Reviews"). The volume ends with a comprehensive bibliography of Sailhamer's published works to encourage you to explore first-hand his insights into God's textual revelation.

# 4

# What Have They Done to My Genesis?

## By John H. Sailhamer

IN THE STORY OF CINDERELLA, domineering stepsisters force a young girl to do the lowliest work in the house—until, that is, Cinderella's true beauty is discovered by the king's son.[1] Her sisters are left dumbfounded. They had never dreamed that others might find Cinderella beautiful, much less that the prince would seek her hand.

This fairy tale came to my mind recently as I watched journalist Bill Moyers lead a discussion on the story of Cain and Abel on the PBS television series *Genesis: A Living Conversation*. It was one of ten free-wheeling discussions carried on by an eclectic group of noted authors, artists, clergy, and scholars that included Muslims, a Buddhist, a Hindu, Jews, agnostics, Catholics, and Protestants. While several later segments included evangelicals, there were none in this episode, titled "The First Murder."

As I watched it, it occurred to me that, as evangelicals, the Bible may be our Cinderella. We have opened our homes to her, but we have relegated her to washing our dishes and scrubbing our floors. We have used her to make our lives theologically comfortable; and she, never one to complain, has remained faithful. But we have been blind to her true loveliness and oblivious to the possibility that others might see real beauty in her. As the series clearly showed, our Cinderella has been to the ball, and the glass slipper has been found. The king's men

---

[1] This article originally appeared in *Christianity Today* 41.1 (January 6, 1997), 46–47. Used by permission.

are now knocking at our door, searching for the beauty they have seen in "our" Scriptures.

### Old Story, New Perspective

Before the series was broadcast, I was prepared to dislike it, anticipating it to be another exercise in the postmodernist deconstruction of our sacred text. To some extent, it was. The participants seemed to read their own agendas into the text while seeking to unite around some nebulous "core religious experience" as reflected in the biblical narratives.

But there was something in the discussion for which I was not prepared—at least, not emotionally. Like evangelicals, they took these stories at face value and saw themselves reflected in the narratives. But they also pressed further for what these stories said to others besides themselves. They were not satisfied until they had thrust upon these texts the full weight of what the story of Cain and Abel meant to all of humanity—especially those who had never, or would never, read it. They wanted to understand the characters in the story, not as believers or saints, but as outsiders, rebels, adversaries.

How differently this familiar story sounded from their perspective! They agonized over the tragic fate of Abel. He did everything right, they noted, but in spite of that, he was killed. That, they insisted, was more troubling than the ostensible brutality of Cain. God shows mercy to Cain, who goes on to build our first city. But Abel is dead. So what hope does the story leave for those like Abel?

I was struck by how seriously they treated the stories. They fought hard to make sense of them and to seek from them some broader meaning for their lives. On the one hand, that made me feel strangely proud of "my" Bible. It was as if something I had cherished all my life had finally been given its due appreciation. But on the other hand, I felt disturbed: Why hadn't the evangelical community, with all its attention to television and media, ever produced such a program? Why did we wait for PBS to present us with a serious, penetrating look at the Book of Genesis?

The answer in part, I believe, is that we evangelicals have become adept at defending the Bible from its adversaries; we have produced a formidable and effective body of literature supporting our case. In the process, however, we have forgotten to ask seriously what it all means. Perhaps we mistakenly assumed that because no one was interested in the stories of the Bible, the stories themselves were uninteresting.

This series challenges Christians like me to a fresh and engaging reading of Scripture. We must look our Cinderella in the face and see her beauty. We must be willing to take her on her own terms—to live in her world, to see our lives as part of her world, and to seek to live according to it. We must not call on her solely to do the menial, and often demeaning, tasks of making our lives apologetically comfortable.

### The Lens of Faith

For me, watching Bill Moyer's conversation was like watching my daughter go off on her first date. While I might have wanted to go with her and hold her hand, I needed to trust her to be her true self. Likewise, when I see the Bible in the hands of unbelievers and agnostics and want to tag along and hold its hand, I must trust the Bible to be itself. As they read it seriously, they open themselves to the inspired Word of God.

If we, in turn, read the same texts with the same liveliness, we will be ready to engage unbelievers in their conversations, bringing to those discussions the clarity of the lens of faith. (The plight of Abel remains unanswerable—unless, of course, a later chapter contains a resurrection and a Heel striking the serpent's head.) Are we ready to read the stories of the Bible with utter seriousness, to think deeply about what they say to us about God and ourselves in a troubled world? Ironically, this is a lesson we can learn a great deal about from Moyers and his friends.

# 5

# Reading the Bible as a Text

## By John H. Sailhamer

I WOULD LIKE TO BEGIN with a personal note about the work of Professor Wolfgang Schneider because I think it illustrates quite well the main point of my reflections in this article.[1] For theological, as well as theoretical reasons, in teaching biblical theology, I have laid great stress in the classroom on the importance of understanding the biblical text as a text. Historical events and the course of history that lies behind the biblical texts are, of course important, but in the last analysis, biblical theology should focus on the biblical text itself. That, at least, is how I have approached the issue.

In approaching theology from such a perspective, I have found an increasing interest and appreciation on the part of students. One could say that over the last 20 years of teaching theology and biblical languages, a veritable sea-change in the interests of students has occurred. Whereas my classes were once filled with students interested in biblical archaeology and geography, I now find them full of students interested in narrative texts and textual strategies. There is little need to convince students of the importance of understanding the text. They are ready and eager to do so. I am not sure where these

---

1 *Ed:* This essay originally appeared in *Narrative and Comment: Contributions to Discourse Grammar and Biblical Hebrew Presented to Wolfgang Schneider*, ed. Eep Talstra (Societas Hebraica Amstelodamensis, 1995), 162–165. Used by permission. The grammar under discussion in this article has since been translated into English: Wolfgang Schneider, *Grammar of Biblical Hebrew*, trans. Randall L. McKinion, Studies in Biblical Hebrew 1 (Peter Lang, 2016).

American and international students are getting such an interest, but I do know it is there.

### I

An awareness of the textual nature of biblical revelation, as well as the appreciation for it, are not the same thing, however, as a thorough understanding of how texts work. My growing interest in texts thus early on left me scurrying for some kind of help in gaining a more theoretical understanding of them. That path first led me in the direction of a general study of text-linguistics and text-theory. Only after some time did I discover that Schneider and others had already applied many of these insights to the Hebrew Bible. By that time I had already begun some initial studies in text-linguistics and the Hebrew Bible and so I was able to compare what I had done with the more comprehensive work of Schneider.

More to the point, however, is the response of my student's to Schneiders's work. For them, Schneider's grammar has represented precisely the tool they had come to expect from Hebrew grammarians but had hitherto not found. I was able to point out to them the shortcomings of traditional grammars such as Gesenius', but they had not received from me the final, comprehensive treatment of biblical Hebrew which was offered by Schneider. In a very practical way Schneider had filled a void, and both the interest and enthusiasm of my students was a testimony to that fact. The overwhelmingly positive response of my students to Schneider's grammar lies at the base of the following reflections on the teaching of biblical exegesis.

Teaching biblical theology and exegesis can have its practical moments as well as its moments of truth. All too frequently these two moments do not happily converge in the classrooms. The practical concerns of the classroom are largely formed around the needs of students. Whatever "truths" we may wish to impart to our students will have to come through the grid of their understanding, not ours. We can, realistically, change their basic thought patterns and perspectives to only a limited extent.

In the 17th century and early 18th centuries, for example, when biblical theology meant the scholastic refinement of dogmatic creeds, theological pedagogy in the academic classroom increasingly busied itself with recasting the discipline into the basically opposite concerns of historicism. The task of theology was thus recast to suit the concerns of the student. The modern notion of biblical theology was born out of just that effort. It was the effort to conceptualize theology as the historical reconstruction of the religion of the individual Israelite.

We know from the study of general cultural trends that such an historical interest was in step with the times of the 19th century. That understanding, of course, clashed with the classical goal of training theologians with the truth of Scripture. Such "truth" most commonly meant the doctrines of the Church. In time, however, the goals of theology and exegesis changed as it attempted to fit the changing needs of the times. By the time theology had caught up with historicism in the classroom, however, the classroom had moved on in the 20th century to the pursuit of idealism, existentialism, and finally, linguistics. In the United States, at least, textuality has become the defining element of our everyday constructs of reality.

II

In the course of redefining itself to fit the classroom, biblical theology and exegesis, which had begun as an adjustment to the prevailing historicism of the 19th century, has become increasingly uneasy, and even uncertain, about its role in raising up the next generation of theologians. It is not, in my opinion, an oversimplification to say that, at present, biblical theology is fundamentally divided over its task. On the one hand, there are those who continue to insist that the task of biblical theology is the reconstruction of the religion of Israel that lies behind the OT texts. On the other hand, there are those who insist that the task of biblical theology lies in articulation of the meaning of the OT texts themselves.

It is my view that the growing needs of the classroom now rests on the side of the latter approach—the meaning of the OT texts. The present generation of theological students, as well as those of the foreseeable future, know what a text is. Though for them it may be primarily a "video text" or "hyper-text," they come to their classes in biblical theology and exegesis with a quite sophisticated understanding of the nature of meaning in texts. They also now understood how such a textual meaning contrasts with classical approaches to the interpretation of historical events. They not only know what the "second naiveté" is, they relish it and understand it to be an essential part of their experience of reality.

To be sure, I am now speaking only of the practical aspects of teaching biblical theology. To many, the lack of interest and importance of history in the classroom is appalling. The truth claims of biblical theology, unlike "virtual reality," for example, are necessarily grounded in historical events. However frightening the prospects are for the apologetic task of the defense of the "truth" of Scripture, there is a bright side to the "new textuality" of today's classroom. Contemporary theological students, unlike many of their predecessors, can readily understand and appreciate the fact that meaning is a function of its own textuality. To understand it, one must view a text in terms of the world which it depicts.

In the case of the Hebrew Bible, that world is not intended to be understood as part of one's own limited experience of the world. In reading Scripture, we are not called to disengage its narrative world to make it fit into our own world. We are, rather, to view our lives, our reality, in terms of its world. The biblical narratives, as Lindbeck puts it, are the "cosmic maps" that provide the grammar with which we learn to articulate the meaning of life and the gospel.[2]

### III

There is, I believe, a direct link between the new textually oriented practical needs of the classroom and the kind of grammar which we find represented in the work of Professor Wolfgang Schneider. Today's students all too easily recognize the inherent fallacies of such standard grammars as Gesenius' Hebrew Grammar. Like the biblical theologians of their own day, Gesenius, Kautzsch, Cowley, and Bergsträsser aimed at reconstructing and articulating the state of affairs that lay behind the biblical text, rather than those in the text itself. The

---

[2] George A. Lindbeck, *The Nature of Doctrine, Religion and Theology in a Postliberal Age* (Westminster Press, 1984).

biblical theologians aimed at reconstructing the religion of Israel. The Hebrew grammarians aimed at reconstructing the language of Israel. Both saw their task as a historical one. Both aimed to show the historical development of their respective objects, religion and language. Both attempted to view their objects within the context of a much broader comparative study, the history of religions and historical linguistics. Both fell victim to the prevailing idealism of the late 19th and early 20th century and its corollaries, textual emendation and neogramarianism. Finally, both failed to see and appreciate the biblical text as an object in its own right—one in need of its own description, rather than a source from which to gather historical evidence.

This is not, of course, to say or imply that classical grammars such as Gesenius's are bereft of linguistic insights. They are, in fact, rich quarries to which we can, and must, continually return. Their use, however, is largely limited to those who are deft enough to traverse them. Still, that is not their chief weakness. Their weakness lies in the fact that they do not look at the text as such in their conceptualizations of grammar. Their focus remains always the language of the text rather than the language in the text. Their goal is the description of the Hebrew language in its various living stages in the past. Moreover, and really the heart of the matter, they assume the form in which we now have the language in the text represents that living stage—or various levels or stages of the living language of ancient Hebrew. The parallel between this view of the language of Scripture and the religion of Israel in biblical theology is striking.

An awareness of the textuality of the Hebrew Bible renders such approaches to grammar not only unwieldy, but also to a large extent obsolete. What the student of Hebrew needs to know is not so much how a nominal clause was used in ancient Hebrew conversation, but how such a clause functions within the strategy of a specific written text. Important theological moments in the biblical text often turn on subtle, but significant, shifts in dialogue as well as changes in the perspective of the narration. Hebrew grammar thus needs to distinguish between parts of texts which move along the narration, that is, those which tell the story (WAYYIQTOL and W/QATAL), and those in which the characters speak and reflect on the events of the story (e.g., YIQTOL and QeTOL).

The student in today's classroom who is interested in textual strategies wants to know how Hebrew narratives begin. What clause structures mark the onset of a new narrative? How do narratives conclude? Where does the emphasis lie within a particular narrative? What does a change in word order imply?

There will always be a place for historical linguistics and a comparative linguistic approach to the Hebrew Bible. It will not, however, serve the new need for a text-oriented grammar such as Schneider's. Changing viewpoints about the nature of the biblical texts and the practical reality of textually competent students has mandated a place for both.

# 6

# Archaeology and the Reliability of the Old Testament

## By John H. Sailhamer

THE TOPIC OF THE HISTORICAL RELIABILITY of the Old Testament (OT) raises two kinds of questions. The first is whether the OT documents have been accurately preserved. Do they represent what their original authors wrote and intended to say? Or, has the OT message somehow been lost in the centuries-long shuffle of copying and re-copying the biblical manuscripts? The second question is whether as modern readers we can rely fully on the historical accuracy of the biblical writings.

The concern for the meaning and accuracy of the OT (Hebrew) manuscripts is the task of biblical Philology, including the related studies of Textual Criticism and the archaeology of ancient Semitic transcriptions. Tasks such as these can be carried out only by highly trained specialists in the Semitic languages of the Bible. The results of such study are indispensable not only for the layperson's confidence in the reliability of the OT, but also for the scholar's defense of that reliability. Much of this work must, understandably, be carried out behind the scenes, unnoticed by lay readers, but under the careful scrutiny of colleagues, evangelical or otherwise. What is at stake in this type of work is nothing less than the historical and scientific grounds for the claims of all Christians that the Bible is a faithful and reliable witness to its original texts and the historical events they record.

Philologists help us lay the foundations for that claim by demonstrating that the Bible we hold in our hands today is the same Bible penned centuries before the birth of Christ. Though such tasks may appear to be dry and arcane, it is helpful to bear in mind that some of our most popular English writers, such as C. S. Lewis and J. R. R. Tolkien, were themselves philologists by profession. What Lewis and Tolkien did for the study of Old English literature, biblical philologists do for the Hebrew manuscripts of the OT. Philology enables us to determine the age of biblical manuscripts and the language in which they are written. It also helps us understand the relationship between biblical Hebrew as a language and the languages of the ancient Near East.

By comparing the biblical texts to ancient documents from the biblical era one learns much about the integrity of the biblical manuscripts and their reliability as witnesses to ancient historical events. Thanks to the contribution of philology to biblical studies, we can confidently say that the biblical Hebrew manuscripts that lie behind our modern English translations give every appearance of being historically linked to authentic ancient Semitic documents from the earliest periods of biblical history.

In 1929, archaeologists uncovered a remarkable cache of clay tablets near the modern region of Ras Shamra, the ancient city of Ugarit, on the northern coast of the Mediterranean Sea. These texts date from the biblical period of the Judges. Some of these tables were found still lying in the ovens where they had been baking at the time the city of Ugarit was destroyed more than 3000 years ago. Of importance to the philologist is the fact that these tablets were written in an ancient Semitic dialect directly related to the language of the Bible. Today that language is called Ugaritic.

An important outcome of this discovery is the evidence it provides for the age and nature of the language of the Bible. It is not a new language, nor is it a language unknown at the time the Bible was written. When the biblical manuscripts are compared with these early Ugaritic tablets, it is evident that the biblical texts have preserved a very ancient form of the language of that period. This is especially true of the poetic texts. They bear all the earmarks of the actual language of the Canaanites during the biblical period. It would have been impossible to imitate or artificially stage the kind of close identity that exists between the language of the OT and that of the early Canaanites of the OT period.

One of the most far reaching archaeological finds of the last half century has been the discovery of what have become known as the Dead Sea Scrolls. These scrolls are the remains of an ancient library of manuscripts stashed away in caves more than 2000 years ago. Of primary interest is the wealth of biblical manuscripts found among these scrolls, most of them dating from the first and second centuries BC. Much has been written about this discovery and much more remains to be written. Needless to say, they cast a great deal of light on the history of the biblical manuscripts. In these texts we have actual manuscripts and parts of manuscripts of the Bible that go back to only a few short centuries from the time of the final composition of many of the books of the Bible. The similarity between these ancient manuscripts and our more recent Hebrew texts shows that the scribes who copied and handled them were as cautious and exacting as modern biblical scholars.

The second question we have raised above regarding archaeology's contribution to the reliability of the OT is whether the historical events recounted in the OT actually happened as they are recounted. Did the biblical authors get it right when they wrote these histories? Here we must lay aside our philological tools and become historians. That means we are faced with the task of reconstructing the events recorded in the Bible and attempting to identify them with known historical events from the ancient Near East. Such comparisons of the OT with ancient history make it possible to measure how close the biblical writers' accounts were to the modern historians' understanding of what "actually happened."

In attempting to get a fix on both biblical and secular historical events, archaeology is of prime importance. After nearly a century of serious digging, biblical archaeologists have reached a broad consensus on how the bits and pieces of the historical puzzle should fit together. In viewing the total picture, the pieces supplied by modern archaeologists fit remarkably well with the picture supplied by the biblical narratives. It is, thus, widely acknowledged that, on balance, the events recorded in the OT Scriptures should not only be taken as historical in the true sense of the term, that is, they actually happened, but also they should be considered as a close, if not exact, replica of the actual events of the ancient world.

Such knowledge of the history of Israel, both in and apart from the Bible, is essential for demonstrating the truthfulness of the biblical account. When we claim the Bible is true, we take that to mean it is historically factual and accurate. But how can we know it is historically accurate without knowing something of the events it is describing? How do we know that biblical history conforms to the events of ancient history unless we know what those events were and how they happened? Before the rise of modern historiography, readers of the Bible were more or less obliged to take the reliability of the Bible at face value. Scriptural reliability and accuracy was a matter of trust in the biblical writers. If the Bible appeared to be making a claim to be historically accurate, being the Word of God, it warranted the reader's trust that it would make such claims with moral integrity. Since Moses wrote the Pentateuch and Moses was a man of integrity, one needn't worry about the accuracy of his work because he could be trusted to tell the truth.

The situation today is quite different. Few today would venture the argument that the OT is historically reliable merely because its authors were morally upright. As important as such an issue may be, it cannot be allowed a central role in biblical apologetics. In today's world, it is expected that biblical truth, in so far as that means historical reliability, must pass through the same fiery trials as other documents claiming to be historical. That means the Bible must often fend for itself in the arena of secular history, and in the face of an historical skepticism that places in doubt not only the central tenets of biblical history, but also any kind of history that involves a faith commitment up front.

The question raised by such a "minimalist" position is how to account for such a sudden change of attitude about not only the Bible's historical reliability but also the reliability of nearly every kind of historical account. Has there been a fundamental change in the field of biblical archaeology? Has there been a surge of new archaeological discoveries which have turned biblical proofs into doubts about the Bible? What has been the source of such negative attacks on both the Bible and history in general? While it may be true that times have changed and new sorts of questions must be asked and answered about the Bible, it is also true that this new attitude about history and the Bible has arisen not out of new evidence about past events, but rather out of deep seated problems that have beset historical research in general. It is in response to such changes in historical method that I want to make the following four observations.

1. The increasingly negative tone of some historians and archaeologists is not the result of new findings or new discoveries at the ancient biblical sites. The fact is that recent discoveries unearthed by archaeologists have continued to produce historical evidence in support of the Bible. In 1993, for example, at the height of the new negativity within scholarly circles, an inscription was unearthed from the 9th Century BC. which mentions the name of David, the first king of the Southern Kingdom. At the same time the new archaeologists were presuming the stories of David to be fiction, this inscription established that David was a real historical figure.

2. The increasingly negative tone of some historians and archaeologists is also not the result of showing that past discoveries of archaeologists were in error. Much of the work of past archaeologists which substantiated the biblical history still stands—in most cases more than ever before. The difference lies in how these earlier discoveries are now interpreted. An example of this comes from one of the most dramatic pieces of historical evidence yet to be uncovered by Egyptologists. It was discovered over a century ago. It is the 13th Century BC. inscription of the Egyptian king Merneptah which mentions a people called "Israel" along with biblical place names such as Canaan and Ashkelon. There could not be a stronger proof of the accuracy of the Bible than this inscription. Here in one of the king's own inscriptions, we have the mention of the people "Israel" by an Egyptian king hundreds of years before modern "minimalist" archaeologists believe there was an Israel.

3. The increasingly negative tone of some historians is the result of a fundamental shift in the way biblical history is conducted. Put simply, according to the biblical "minimalists," the biblical record cannot and should not play a role in reconstructing biblical history. It is, of course, valuable to view ancient history without an undue emphasis on the Bible. There are many persons and events in the ancient world not mentioned in the Bible. The problem, however, is that after these archaeologists have reconstructed the biblical history without

the biblical text, they go on to accuse the Bible of getting it wrong because it does not conform to their newly reconstructed version of that history. The fact is, the only other written history of ancient Israel ever available comes from the Bible. They, thus, judge the biblical version against their own version of its history. One would think the Bible should at least be allowed to speak on its behalf and give its own version of the events it records. Both versions, the biblical one and the secular one, should be evaluated against the available evidence.

To give one example, the archaeological starting point of the history of the dynasty of David and Solomon has always been the remains of monumental structures from the 10th Century BC. These structures were dated to this period because it was assumed they were related to the kingdoms of David and Solomon, which the Bible credits with the origin of the monarchy. Without the biblical picture by which to evaluate the archaeological remains, these monumental structures could also be dated to the 9th Century and hence, to the time after David and Solomon. With such a view of the evidence, it would appear that the actual origins of the great Israelite monarchy came after the time of David and Solomon. The Bible thus appears to be a hundred years off target. But, it is only by discounting the biblical record in the first place that these historians are able to conclude the Bible has mixed up its dates. If the Bible is allowed to speak for itself, it conforms without a hitch to the existing archaeological evidence.

4. The last observation is complex, but it lies at the heart of the debate over history and the Bible. What the new historians and archaeologists are often saying is that their evidence sometimes contradicts what earlier archaeologists said about the Bible. Put this way, it is not a question of the historical reliability of the Bible as much as it is a question of the historical reliability of the work of earlier archaeologists. The question is not so much whether the Bible is true as it is whether the dominant theories of great biblical archaeologists were true. What often goes unsaid in these debates is that sometimes, in order to get their facts to fit the Bible, earlier archaeologists (such as William F. Albright) made assumptions about biblical history that contradicted the Bible itself. The negative work of the new archaeologists therefore can lend valuable support to biblical history by undermining previous false assumptions about that history.

The past generation of archaeologists, under the leadership of Albright, for example, unanimously assumed that Israel's exodus from Egypt occurred during the time of the 19th Dynasty in Egypt under the reign of Ramesses II. Based on that chronology, earlier historians and archaeologists assumed the Bible to be in error when it recorded the destruction of the city of Jericho by the Israelites. Jericho, they argued, was destroyed more than a century before the Israelites left Egypt and entered Canaan. According to their chronology, Jericho was already in ruins by the time Israel had left Egypt. If they had followed the biblical chronology, however, it would have placed the exodus in the time of the 18th dynasty, more than a century earlier and at roughly the time of the destruction of Jericho. There is, thus, often a need for a correction, not of the Bible, but of the assumed results of earlier historical reconstructions.

The study of history and biblical archaeology is a complex task. The bottom line in the above observations is that the new archaeologists (minimalists) are sometimes guilty of passing on their judgments about biblical history without considering all the evidence. No one is suggesting they must take the Bible as true in order to use it in reconstructing biblical history. They should, however, take the Bible seriously as at least one version of that history worthy of consideration and evaluation.

To be sure, attempts to rethink the results of past work are admirable. While much of it might be called "revisionist" history, some of it may represent a serious attempt to look at the evidence in a new light. Biblical minimalists, however, are wrong in discounting the biblical narratives as part of the evidence. Biblical narratives as a whole cannot always be treated as eyewitness accounts. Much of the book of Kings, for example, records events several hundred years earlier than the time of its composition. That does not mean that these narratives are spun out of thin air.

Here is where evangelicals may serve a valuable (if unappreciated) purpose in the larger scheme of things. They, as few others, are prepared to take these biblical texts at face value and ask how they fit into what historians and archaeologists tell us happened.

# 7

# Cosmic Maps, Prophecy Charts, and the Hollywood Movie: A Biblical Realist Looks at the Eclipse of Old Testament Narrative

By John H. Sailhamer

## 1. Introduction

THERE IS A GENERAL RECOGNITION TODAY that our society has lost its identity.[1] It has lost its sense of a common story. Recently in a television interview, Ken Burns, the writer and producer of the PBS series "Baseball," was asked why he chose to devote such time and attention to the game of baseball. His answer was surprising, but insightful. Baseball, he said, is the only common story that Americans still share. A generation ago, Americans had a much more comprehensive story. That story was rooted in a shared experience. It was, moreover, founded upon a common religious heritage. That heritage was, in fact, a continuation of the biblical story. With the collapse of that story, however, the only remaining thread in the common bond of American society is now baseball. Thus Ken Burns, the PBS producer, set out to tell the story of baseball. It was an effort, he said, to bring our country together.

Without a story to define us as a nation, we cease to act as a nation and, really, cease to be a nation. I think we would all agree that the loss of our nation's story is a serious problem today and affects every part of life. There is, however, an even more serious loss of story. The Christian Church also has a story. That story is told in the Bible. To the

---

[1] *Ed:* This article represents the two lectures read for the annual Criswell Theological Lecture, February, 1995. It originally appeared in *Criswell Theological Review* 7.2 (1994): 65–81. Used by permission.

extent that our individual stories are linked to the biblical story, our lives have meaning and purpose. If we should ever lose that story, or if that story should be changed in any way, we will quickly forget who we are. One of the central tasks of Christian education is to ensure that the biblical story continues to be told. An equally important task is to ensure that the story is preserved intact. It is my contention that the biblical story is in danger today of being distorted, accommodated, changed, and ignored. Some of those pressures are exerted by the Bible's own best friends.

## 2. The Biblical Story

I want to address the issue of the biblical story. I want to talk about what makes it tick. Why is it so important? What threatens it today?

As my title suggests, I want to approach the biblical story under three headings: 1) cosmic maps; 2) prophecy charts, and; 3) the Hollywood movie. These three headings, I think, point to, or at least illustrate, the essential function of the biblical story. That function is to give us a sense of the nature and purpose of God's world. In the words of N. Goodman, the biblical story is a "way of worldmaking."[2]

### 2.1. "Cosmic Maps"

Let's begin by looking at "cosmic maps." I am taking the idea of a "cosmic map" from the Yale theologian George Lindbeck. In his book, *The Nature of Doctrine,* Lindbeck addresses the question of the nature of religion and theology in a "post-liberal" age. What he means by a post-liberal age is that in his view classical liberalism has come to an end. We live in an age which has come to appreciate the essential limitations, indeed fallacies, of classical liberalism. Liberalism was born out of the Enlightenment notion that reason, or human experience, is the ultimate source of truth. Religion, according to the Enlightenment and modern liberalism, consists of a basic "core experience" of reality. Every human being has such a "core experience," or at least is capable of having one. Theology is the specific, culturally conditioned expression given to one's "core experience."

---

2 Nelson Goodman, *Ways of Worldmaking* (Hackett Publishing Company, 1978).

Religion and theology are like the eruption of a volcano. The core molten lava of religious experience breaks through the crust of the earth's surface at various places and forms a volcano. A whole ecological system then forms around the volcano. That system is analogous to theology. Liberalism's view of the religion and theology of the Bible, for example, is that the biblical story is Israel's expression of their "core experience." Christianity is also a volcano that has broken through the earth's surface at a particular time and place. Liberalism leads to pluralism because all "religions" are merely the cultural-bound theological articulations of a common "core experience." Behind all religions lies the same deep structural "core experience." All religions are expressions of the same basic truth.

Lindbeck argues that liberalism is simply wrong. There are no universal "core experiences." That is not the way cultures and religions work. What we know about religions today, says Lindbeck, suggests another, quite different, explanation. Religion is an essential feature of culture. Religion is a component of culture in the same sense as language is a component of culture. Religion and language are what create the basic semantic structures of culture. They are not created by culture. They create culture. Language gives a culture its essential surface structures of meaning. It defines for a culture the ways it organizes its world—both the physical world and the world of its ideas. Religion gives a culture its essential deep structures of meaning. Religion tells a culture what is real and not real, what is true and what is false, what is good and what is evil. Religion tells a culture what lies behind the world defined for it by language. Religion tells a culture about the nature of God, humanity, sin, and redemption. Religion gives a culture the grammar with which it seeks to express itself.

In other words, for Lindbeck, there are no common "core experiences," at least not any that can serve as a meaningful deep structure. Religions, like individual languages, have their own distinct idioms. Each religion has its own unique way of defining human experience. There are no common deep structures. Human experiences are essentially semantically neutral until they are refracted through a particular religious prism. Within cultures, faith and religion serve as interpretive schemes which, like language, a culture uses to give meaning to human experience. "Religions are seen as comprehensive interpretive schemes, usually embodied in . . . narratives . . . which structure human experience and understanding of self and world."[3] Thus the biblical narratives and their story, as Lindbeck sees it, are "similar to a (linguistic) idiom that makes possible the description of realities, the formulation of beliefs, and the experiencing of inner attitudes, feelings, and sentiments . . . it is a communal phenomenon that shapes the subjectivities of individuals rather than being primarily a manifestation of those subjectivities."[4]

To become religious in such a scheme "involves becoming skilled in the language, the symbol system of a given religion. To become a Christian involves learning the story of Israel and of Jesus well enough to interpret and experience oneself and one's world in its terms."[5] In the model of culture suggested by Lindbeck, the biblical story is the language of a culture which gives common shape and meaning to human experience. How does it do this? Lindbeck argues (and I agree) that the Bible structures culture (whatever culture) by means of its narratives. The biblical narratives are a "cosmic map." They are the comprehensive interpretive scheme which shows the fundamental structures of reality. What is true, good, and real in the biblical narratives are, in fact, what are to be taken as true, good, and real. The world we experience as readers of the Bible is the only real world.

To be true and real, our own individual world must conform to the world we read about in the Bible. It is no accident that the Bible opens with the statement, "In the beginning God created the heavens and the earth." The Bible begins with the one and only reality that preceded its world, that is, God. God alone exists eternally. All else is dependent on him and owes its origin to him. From that starting point the

---

3   Lindbeck, *Nature of Doctrine*, 32.
4   Lindbeck, *Nature of Doctrine*, 33.
5   "A religion is above all an external word, a verbum externum, that molds and shapes the self and its world, rather than an expression or thematization of a preexisting self or of preconceptual experience. The verbum internum (traditionally equated by Christians with the action of the Holy Spirit) is also crucially important, but it would be understood in a theological use of the model as a capacity for hearing and accepting the true religion, the true external word, rather than as a common experience diversely articulated in different religions" (Lindbeck, *Nature of Doctrine*, 34).

Bible begins to unfold its cosmic map. From that point the Bible begins to define what is real and what is not real, what is true and what is false, what is good and what is evil. Like the lexicon and grammar of a language, the Bible gives shape and meaning to our world by presenting it to us as a totality.

An important aspect of Lindbeck's view of culture and religion is the active role which the biblical narratives play in defining the nature of reality. "Human experience," says Lindbeck,

> is shaped, molded, and in a sense constituted by cultural and linguistic forms. There are numberless thoughts we cannot think, sentiments we cannot have, and realities we cannot perceive unless we learn to use the appropriate symbol systems. A comprehensive scheme or story used to structure all dimensions of existence is not primarily a set of propositions to be believed, but is rather the medium in which one moves, a set of skills that one employs in living one's life. Thus while a religion's truth claims are often of the utmost importance to it (as in the case of Christianity), it is, nevertheless, the conceptual vocabulary and the syntax or inner logic which determine the kinds of truth claims the religion can make.[6]

What Lindbeck is getting at here, I think, is that the Bible, and particularly its narrative, creates and defines for us the fundamental nature of the world in which we live. It is within that world that the Gospel makes sense. The Bible provides the "cosmic map" within which the lost can see that they are lost and also by which they can find their way home. Central to the biblical world is the need of redemption and the possibility of atonement.

I would now like to turn to three personal ways in which my own "cosmic map" has been formed. In some respects, I am representative of many in my generation. In other ways I am not. I give these examples from my own personal experience because they provide an illustration of how "cosmic maps" work, and ultimately, how the Bible structures our reality.

---

6 Lindbeck, *Nature of Doctrine*, 34-35.

## 2.2. How Are "Cosmic Maps" Formed?
## Three Examples from My Own Personal Experience

### 2.2.1. Prophecy Charts

When I was growing up, my father was a pastor and an evangelist. In our church we used to have what was called a "prophecy chart" hanging in the front of the sanctuary. That prophecy chart was one of my first "cosmic maps." It was a rather conspicuous one at that. It was a large piece of painted canvas – like a banner. It had seven circles drawn on it, each representing one of the dispensations noted in the Scofield Bible. At either end of the chart there was a half-circle which represented "eternity past" and "eternity future." In the middle of these two parts of eternity there stood all of human history. At the end of history stood the "Great Tribulation," the "Millennium," the "Great White Throne Judgment," and the "Lake of Fire." It was not difficult in that church to know the "big picture." It was also very clear where we, as a church and as individuals, stood within that picture. In every prophecy chart I had ever seen, we were only about 6 inches from the "Lake of Fire." I know for me, as a young child, that prophecy chart had a powerful influence on my life. It was like a map at the shopping mall. I always knew exactly where I was in God's program. I learned to watch and wait for God's next act in history. It scared me, and at the same time, it gave me comfort. I learned how to live my life "in light of the second coming of Christ."

There is a book out today about such churches and about growing up with such expectations. It is called "Living in the Shadow of the Second Coming." It is an interesting book, but, to be honest, I do not like the title. For me, at least, and I know I speak for those in my church, the second coming did not cast a shadow upon our lives. The second coming cast a bright light of hope. It made every day of my young life meaningful. It gave it direction and purpose. There was anticipation. And there was also a constant warning: Maybe today! Our youth director would say to us, "Would you like to be doing that when Christ returns?" or "Would you like to be in a movie theater when the Lord returns?" I have to be honest, when I look back. Without such warnings my life would not have been the same.

Now let me quickly say that I do not think we should start hanging prophecy charts in our churches again. It was, admittedly, a quite unsophisticated way to create a "cosmic map." But it was effective. We got the point. Now that I have four children of my own, I often ask myself, What has replaced the prophecy chart for my children? How are they learning about God's plan for the ages, the whole counsel of God, and what the prophets say? Do they know down deep how their lives fit into God's plan? Do they know what God's plan is? A Christian's life is like a piece of a jigsaw puzzle. We need to see how we fit into the whole picture. The contours and colors of our lives, like a piece of a jigsaw puzzle, are meaningless without a sense of God's big picture. The prophecy chart once did that for many of us. I do not think it could do it again. Something, however, must take its place.

### 2.2.2. The Hollywood Movie

I turn now to the second way in which I have been given a "cosmic map"—the Hollywood Movie. Throughout all of my growing up years, I was not allowed to "go to movies." Movies were not allowed. There were only two exceptions: movies with biblical themes (10 Commandments, David and Bathsheba) and "old movies" on TV. Leaving aside the matter of movies with biblical themes (which is a different subject altogether), let me say that growing up in Southern California in the late 1950s, I saw a lot of "old movies." Through luck or providence, my family moved to California just at the time when KHJ-TV purchased the entire film library of RKO Studios from Howard Hughes. That began what was then called the "Fabulous 52" series. For 52 weeks each year, KHJ-TV ran a classic Hollywood movie every night of the week and several times over the weekend. I spent many a night, many a week, watching the same classic Hollywood movie over and over again. According to Lindbeck, What was happening to me? Hollywood was giving me a "cosmic map." It was a "cosmic map" made of old reruns, but it was a powerful statement about the world, the good, the bad, the true, the false—it carefully and precisely defined for me the reality of the 30's and 40's as Hollywood had seen it. That "cosmic map" was, to be sure, a sort of hand-me-down. But it was a powerful map of reality. There was in those movies, at least in my life, stiff competition between the prophecy chart and Hollywood.

In the 20th century, the role of the movies and television, and now videos, has been central in defining our "cosmic maps." Reality, for many, if not most 20th century Americans, has been defined by the movies and television. Lucy and Ricky Ricardo, Fred and Ethel Mertz, June and Ward Cleaver—these families sometimes have more reality than our next door neighbors. A few year ago my wife, Patty, was in the teacher's lounge of her school. She overheard some teachers talking about another woman whom she did not know. The teachers were talking about all the troubles this woman had gone through. Her family problems, her health problems, her problems at work. Finally my wife broke into their conversation and asked, in a compassionate tone which showed she was concerned, "Who is this lady?" The teachers broke out in laughter. They laughed because the woman they were talking about was one of the characters in a soap opera they had been watching. Their conversation about her was just as if she were a real person.

The noted film critic Neal Gabler has written an intriguing study of the Hollywood film industry. He has entitled the book, *An Empire of their Own*.[7] Gabler's thesis is that the view of American life and of the world which we know as the classic Hollywood film (e.g., "It's a Wonderful Life") was, and is (as we might expect), a view of a world that never really existed. The world of the classic Hollywood movie was, in reality, merely the world which the Hollywood movie producers created from their own imagination. Gabler's thesis is that those Hollywood producers created their world primarily, and principally, for themselves. It was a world which reflected the kind of world they themselves wanted to live in but could not.

Most Hollywood producers at that time were immigrants to this country. Their movies presented the world of the "American Dream" which they had sought in coming to this country, but it was a world which they had not found when they got here. As immigrants in the early part of this century, they had been excluded from the "real America" whatever it might have been. Thus, having no place else to go, says Gabler, they created their own "American Dream." They created an

---

7 Neal Gabler, *An Empire of their Own* (Crown Pub., 1988).

"Empire of their own." It is that dream, that world, which we know so well from the Hollywood movies. Louis Mayer, the head of MGM and the most powerful man in Hollywood at the time, spent most of his waking hours watching the movies he had produced. He watched "old movies" just like I did. That was his world just as it was quickly becoming mine.

It would be interesting and tempting to diverge from our topic and discuss just what the "world" created by the Hollywood movie was like. It would also be fun to point out how "biblical" such a world really was. The major producers in Hollywood during its heyday, for example, were all fundamentally influenced by the stories of the Bible. The greatest Hollywood producer of all time, D. W. Griffith, was quite biblically literate. In Griffith's scenes of Babylon in the classic silent film "Intolerance," for example, Hollywood and the prophecy chart, in fact, merge into a single image. That is true of many Hollywood films. The book has not yet been written (that I know of) on the relationship between Hollywood and modern American evangelicalism.

I must move on, now, to my third example of how my own "cosmic map" was formed. I call this "the old fashion way"—by reading it.

*2.2.3. Reading the Bible*

A good friend of mine recently offered a probing observation about me. It was an observation that you could tell was really a form of question. He had heard me talk about my upbringing and my father and his prophecy charts. He could see I had a deep appreciation for my heritage. He could also see I had gone quite a way beyond the rather simplistic observations of those prophecy charts and prophetic sermons of my father. His question was, How could I still have an appreciation for prophecy charts? That, for me, was not a hard question to answer. I told him that things like a prophecy chart were of great value in my life because they pointed me back to the Bible's own story. They forced me to return to the Bible and read it again. They helped me read it as well. They helped me see the "big picture." They helped me see the things which Christians in all ages had seen in Scripture. They helped me see the hand of God in the course of human history—a human history whose outline was given in Scripture itself. It was a history that followed the outline of Daniel's visions and would come to a close in the visions of St. John.

To be sure, I have been able to fill in and enrich my understanding of the Bible many times over through my own study and reading of Scripture. Nevertheless, when I read the great theologians of the Church, Augustine, Luther, Calvin, Cocceius, and others, I find the grasp which these men and women had of the whole counsel of God was very near that picture of God's plan for the ages which my father's prophecy chart had given me. The details, for sure, were different, and we may dispute about the details. But the plan itself, was essentially that of Augustine, Luther, Calvin—not to mention the Apostle Paul and St. John. That, of course, was not an accident. Not only did those who drew up prophecy charts read and reread their Bibles. They also stood on the shoulders of many others who searched the Scriptures. They were, in fact, a part of a long line of biblical scholars which can be traced back to the classical writers of the 16th and 17th centuries.

My father was not a biblical scholar. His teachers in Bible School were not scholars. In many cases, in fact, they had an aversion to real scholarship. But whether they knew it or not, their understanding of Scripture was rooted in some of the best biblical scholarship ever produced by the Church—here I have in mind the works of Bengel, Vitringa, Cocceius, and Crusius, the unsung heroes of modern evangelicalism. I was enriched much further than my father ever imagined when he hung that rather crude and unsophisticated prophecy chart at the front of our Church sanctuary.

What I am saying is that the effect which my Bible background had on me was to point me to the biblical text. Through reading the Bible I had been given a biblical, that is, textual "cosmic map." I had something, though in a very simple way, which the prophets, the apostles, and the great theologians of the Church had themselves cherished. I had a world that was fundamentally informed and structured by the Scriptures. I had the heritage of all 20th century evangelicals—the heritage of Scripture. I had the privilege to grow up among a people who held the Bible to be God's Word, and who understood its "world" to be the only real world.

Then something very different happened to me. I graduated from college and went to seminary. From that experience I nearly lost it all.

That is, I nearly lost my biblical "cosmic map." I nearly lost it, not because seminary was a challenge or a threat to my faith. The reason I say I nearly lost my "cosmic map" at seminary is because it was there that I got the idea of going to graduate school and studying ancient Near East history. It was not that the study of ancient history threatened my biblical cosmic map. It was because it threatened to replace my map with another quite different one. As I now look back on it, the point where my biblical "cosmic map" was "almost lost" was at the point where the idea entered my head that the study of ancient near East history would help me understand the Bible. Thus it was to understand the Bible that I went off to study the ancient Near East. For me personally it was a very fortunate thing indeed that the same year I entered graduate school, Yale University Press saw fit to publish a book written by Hans Frei entitled *The Eclipse of Biblical Narrative*.[8] It was that book which rescued my biblical "cosmic map." Frei's book was not written to evangelicals, nor did he even have evangelicalism in mind when he wrote the book. The book does speak, however, to crucial issues which face evangelicals today.

In his book, Frei has addressed the question of where the locus of meaning lies in biblical narrative. His central focus is on the way biblical narratives contribute to our "cosmic maps." How do they produce meaning for us in our world?

It is Frei's contention that the Bible's purpose is to produce meaning by creating a meaningful world for us with its narrative. It does this by putting before our eyes a world in which Jesus and the Gospels make sense. Like a Hollywood movie, the Bible creates an empire of its own. The key difference between the two, however, is that while the Hollywood movie does not claim to be real, the Bible does. Biblical narrative is realist narrative—it presents persons and events as real persons and real events and it expects us to treat them as such. To understand the Bible one must approach it on its own terms. That means one must accept its world as the only true reality and attempt to understand one's own life within the context of that world. The Bible expects us to come into its world. To attempt to force the Bible into another world is to miss the whole purpose for which the Bible

---

8 Hans W. Frei, *The Eclipse of Biblical Narrative: A Study in Eighteenth and Nineteenth Century Hermeneutics* (Yale University Press, 1974).

was written. Here, we will see, is the crux of the matter. Do we accept the Bible and its world or do we make it fit into another world, the world which has been created by modern historical research? That is, the world of the ancient Near East?

According to Frei, the biblical narratives were correctly and profoundly appreciated in times past. Biblical scholars, such as Calvin and Augustine, clearly understood the Bible's intent. They let its world become their own. They accepted the Bible's world as the only real world. The Bible was correctly understood, not because these older biblical scholars were brighter or more learned. The Bible was understood correctly because earlier biblical scholars and readers simply accepted the presentations of the biblical narratives as real and true. Before the rise of historical criticism in the 17th and 18th centuries, Frei argues, the Bible was read literally and historically as a true and accurate account of God's acts in real historical events. It was assumed that the realism of the biblical narratives was in fact an indication that the biblical authors had described historical[9] events just as they had happened.[10]

This description of one's reading the Bible seems quite natural to evangelicals. It has, in fact, fallen to the lot of evangelicalism to preserve this reading of the biblical narratives. According to such an understanding of the Bible, the real world is identified as the world actually described in the Bible and one's own world is meaningful only insofar as it can be viewed as part of the world of the Bible. On this

---

9 Frei suggests that these early theologians were mistaken in their understanding of the biblical narratives and that the realism of the narratives was intended only to be "history-like," not real history. Sternberg, we believe correctly, takes issue with Frei on this important point. According to Sternberg, Frei has unduly limited the aim of biblical realism to a merely literary device. Frei "wishes to focus attention on the biblical text by cutting through the hopeless tangle that religious controversy has made of the issues of inspiration and history. But instead of suspending judgment on them as articles of faith... he tries to neutralize them altogether." Meir Sternberg, *The Poetics of Biblical Narrative* (Indiana University Press, 1985), 82.

10 Western Christian reading of the Bible in the days before the rise of historical criticism in the 18th century was usually strongly realistic, i.e., at once literal and historical, and not only doctrinal and edifying. The words and sentences meant what they said, and because they did so they accurately described real events and real truths that were rightly put only in those terms and no others. Frei, *Eclipse*, 1.

point, Frei acknowledges his dependence on Erich Auerbach's description of the real world in biblical narrative,

> The world of the Scripture stories is not satisfied with claiming to be a historically true reality—it insists that it is the only real world. ... All other scenes, issues, and ordinances have no right to appear independently of it, and it is promised that all of them, the history of all mankind, will be given their due place within its frame.[11]

What this means is that in these earlier views, the Bible had meaning because it described real and meaningful events. Moreover, these events fit together in a meaningful whole. It was a whole world created and sustained by a sovereign God. The concept of divine providence was, in fact, the matting that held together the depiction of events in the biblical narratives and the occurrence of those events in history. God was the author of both the Bible and the historical events which the Bible depicts. As Meir Sternberg has put it, "With God postulated as double author, the biblical narrator can enjoy the privileges of art without renouncing his historical titles."[12]

The medieval theologian, Thomas Aquinas (*Summa Theologica*), has given the Church its definitive expression of this idea: (Aquinas said) "The author of Scripture is God, in whose power it is not only to use words for making known his will (which any human being is able to do), but also historical events in the real world."[13] For Thomas, the course of human events was a real story written by God in the real world. "History" is "His story." This is precisely the biblical view described above by Auerbach. Frei calls such a reading of the biblical narratives "precritical." It is precritical because it takes the Bible at face value and reads it as it was intended. It is also precritical because it represents the viewpoint of most biblical scholars before the rise of historical criticism. The key element in the precritical view of the Bible and history is divine providence. What Thomas has described is

---

11  Erich Auerbach, *Mimesis: The Representation of Reality in Western Literature*, trans. Willard R. Trask (Princeton University Press, 1953).

12  Sternberg, *Poetics*, 82.

13  "*Respondeo dicendum, quod auctor sacrae Scripturae est Deus, in cujus potestate est, ut non solum voces ad significandum accommodet (quod etiam homo facere potest) sed etiam res ipsas.*" Thomas Aquinas, *Summa Theologica* (Forzan, 1894), 25.

the convergence of the biblical record of events with God's providential work of bringing those events to pass. The Bible describes the very events that happened just as they happened.

Frei argues that over the last two centuries, the precritical understanding of Scripture has been gradually eroded by an increasingly historical reading of the Bible. We have grown accustomed to looking for biblical meaning beyond the narratives themselves and within the events they recorded. The aim of biblical interpretation ceased being the narrative texts and began to focus on the process of reconstructing "what really happened" in the actual historical events. The meaning of the Bible was not that which the Bible depicted but that which really happened.

But how do we know what really happened, apart from the Bible? We know what really happened by applying the tools of historical research. History tells us what really happened. History tells us the meaning of the events that lie behind the biblical narratives. As a result of this shift in focus from the text to the event, biblical scholars paid less attention to the text as such and devoted an increasing amount of attention to reconstructing historical events. It is this deflection of attention away from the text and onto the events of history which Frei speaks of as an "eclipse" of the biblical narrative.

According to Frei, one can see most clearly[14] the theologians' shift in attitude toward the biblical narratives in the nature of their response to the challenge of English Deism in the 18th century.[15] On two

---

14 Frei argues that the origin of the "eclipse" of biblical narrative had already begun to occur in the middle of the 17th century with the works of Johannes Coccejus (*Eclipse*, 46–50). In his attempt to link biblical prophecy to events in his own day, Coccejus frequently identified the meaning of the prophetic message with contemporary historical events. The mourning spoken of in Isa 33:7, for example, is identified by Coccejus as a reference to the death of the Swedish king, Gustavus Adolphus: *Haec optimè conveni-unt in Gustavum Adolphum.*

15 Klaus Scholder has argued, and Frei agrees, that the breakdown of the link between the biblical world and the world view of modern man had begun to take hold much earlier, "In der Auseinandersetzung mit dem neuen Wirklichkeitsverständnis, das von den ersten Jahrzehnten des 17. Jahrhunderts an immer entschiedener auftritt, das immer deutlicher dem biblischen Weltund Menschenbild in seiner traditionellen Überlieferung widerspricht und diesen Widerspruch mit immer unwiderleglicheren Beweisen bekräftigt, entstehen die ersten Versuche der historischen Kritik, mit denen die historischkritische Theologie ihren Anfang nimmt." *Ursprünge und Probleme der*

important points Deism challenged the precritical attitude toward Scripture. First, Deism rejected outright the notion of divine providence. Deism held that the universe was guided by its own internal and universal laws and that the will of God was not a direct factor in its operation. Secondly, Deism rejected the idea of special revelation. God had not broken into the web of causes and effects to express His will directly to human beings. History ran its own course and followed its own laws. God had not disturbed the flow of history to insert his own special revelation. One cannot imagine a more frontal attack on the biblical "cosmic map" than Deism presented. Divine providence and special revelation lie at the center of the biblical view of the world.

The loss of the notion of divine providence, Frei argues, meant there was no longer any certainty in the course of history. How could we be sure that the course of God's acts in history were adequately reflected in the course those actions followed in the scriptural narratives? The link which Aquinas had seen between the things that happened in history and the description of them in the Bible was broken. God was no longer the author of either Scripture or history.[16]

The loss of such a link meant that the task of describing the relationship between God's acts in history and the record of those acts in Scripture passed from exegesis into the domain of historical science. Whereas previously one could turn to scriptural exegesis to learn about God's acts in history, now one must resort to a scientific and historical reconstruction of the events themselves. History, rather than the text of Scripture, had thus become the central focus for understanding the meaning of Scripture. History and science were now the source of the biblical "cosmic map."

---

*Bibelkritik im 17. Jahrhundert. Ein Beitrag zur Entstehung der historisch-kritischen Theologie* (Chr. Kaiser Verlag, 1966), 9.

16 Scholder maintained, "If the historical-critical theology is characterized by the fact that it has come to grips fundamentally and methodologically with the modern understanding of the world, then its origins must be linked with the rise of the new, modern world view.... From this very fact also is revealed the route whereby we may understand the origin of historical criticism. It must have begun just at the point where the modern view of reality reached its full form, that is, where the older unity of the Scriptures, the world view and faith became problematic..." (*Ursprünge und Probleme*, 9).

As I have already suggested, Frei did not write his book with evangelicals in mind. On at least one occasion, Frei was given the opportunity to respond to the specific issues of evangelicalism. On that occasion, Frei politely declined the offer. In spite of his reluctance to speak to the issues of evangelicalism, Frei's basic insight still deserves an evangelical response. On numerous occasions, I have attempted to give such a response. Here I want only to summarize the main points I have tried to make. First, I believe evangelicals today are running the risk of eclipsing the biblical text in a way similar to its eclipse at the hands of historical criticism. Evangelicals have rightly stressed the importance of history in demonstrating the accuracy and reliability of the biblical narratives. A knowledge of historical background information, for example, can serve that purpose. Here, however, evangelicals must exercise an appropriate caution. Historical information has an apologetic value. Historical information must not, however, take the place of the meaning of the text.

Let me give one example. In Exod 7:20, "Moses and Aaron did just as the LORD had commanded. He raised his staff in the presence of Pharaoh and his officials and struck the water of the Nile, and all the water was changed into blood. The fish in the Nile died, and the river smelled so bad that the Egyptians could not drink its water. Blood was everywhere in Egypt." The intent of the narrative appears clear enough – "all the water was changed into blood." Moses raised his staff (A) - · the water of the Nile became Blood (B) - · the fish in the Nile died and the Egyptians could not drink the water (C).

The realism of earlier biblical commentators led them to take this statement at face value. It meant that the waters of the river actually became blood: the biblical narrative (A – · B – · C) was identical with the historical event (A – · B – · C). Henry Ainsworth, for example, explains the text in the following manner; (he says) "as the Egyptians had shed the blood of the children of *Israel*, drowning them in the river, Exod 1:22, so in this first plague, God rewardeth that, by turning their waters into blood."[17] The seriousness with which the earlier commentators read this narrative as real history can be seen in the remarks of Cornelius a Lapide:

---

17 Henry Ainsworth, *Annotations upon the Second Booke of Moses Called Exodus* (M. Parsons, 1639), 23.

It should be noted that there was not merely one miracle here but many, or rather, one continuous conversion of the flowing waters of the Nile into blood which happened for seven days. For the Nile in Ethiopia bore pure waters, but when they reached the borders of Egypt, the water immediately turned into blood persistently and continuously throughout the seven days The waters did not merely have the color of blood, but they also had the nature of blood and were, in fact, really blood.[18]

Later conservative, and more "historically" oriented commentators, began to understand the sense of this passage within the context of a growing historical consciousness. They retained a miraculous element, but understood the meaning of the text in light of historical analogies. They wanted the biblical world to fit into their own world, or the world they imagined the ancient Near Eastern world to be.

Keil, for example, says of the passage, "The changing of the water into blood is to be interpreted in the same sense as in Joel iii. 4, where the moon is said to be turned into blood; that is to say, not as a chemical change into real blood, but as a change in the colour, which caused it to assume the appearance of blood (2 Kings 3:22)."[19] Keil then gives the basis for this interpretation and we can see his dependence on the principle of historical analogy:

> According to the statements of many travellers, the Nile water changes its colour when the water is lowest, assumes first of all a greenish hue and is almost undrinkable, and then, while it is rising, becomes as red as ochre, when it is more wholesome again. The causes of this change have not been sufficiently investigated. The reddening of the water is attributed by many to the red earth, which the river brings down ... but Ehrenberg came to the

---

18 Cornelius a Lapide, (d. 1637) "Ubi nota, non unum hic fuisse miraculum, sed multa, vel potius unum continuatum, per continuam aquarum Nili affluentium in sanguinem conversionem, idque per septem dies. Nam Nilus in /Ethiopia puras ferebat aquas; ubi vero attingebat fines /Egypti, mox vertebatur in sanguinem, idque assidue et continuo per septem dies—aquae non tantum colorem, sed et naturam habebant sanguinis, erantque verus sanguis" (*Commentarla in Scripturam Sacram*).

19 C. E Keil, *Biblical Commentary on the Old Testament*, Vol. 1 (Eerdmans, 1971), 478.

conclusion, after microscopical examinations, that it was caused by cryptogamic plants and infusoria. This natural phenomenon was here intensified into a miracle, not only by the fact that the change took place immediately in all the branches of the river at Moses' word and through the smiting of the Nile, but even more by a chemical change in the water, which caused the fishes to die, the stream to stink, and, what seems to indicate putrefaction, the water to become undrinkable ... [20]

The point of this discussion is that in these evangelical conservative commentaries, the meaning of the biblical text ("the water became blood") *is not* taken as ostensibly true but rather is identified with the meaning of the event as it has been reconstructed from similar events ("the water became red *like* blood"). The miraculous element in the first plague is retained but it is nevertheless significantly reduced to that of an intensification of a natural phenomenon—red algae. Moreover, the narrative link between the blood of the Hebrew children thrown into the Nile in Exodus 1 and the Nile becoming blood is lost. The text thus loses an important clue to its meaning.

It is not hard to see how such a shift effects the meaning of the biblical text. Once the meaning of revelation in the Bible becomes identified with *that which we think actually happened,* the focus becomes the meaning of the historical event as such. The text says the Nile became blood but we think it more likely that it became red like blood with algae. Hence, the goal of Bible study becomes the theological meaning of *what we think actually happened.* Or at least what the

---

[20] Keil, *Biblical Commentary on the Old Testament,* 478-79. More recently, Kaiser has taken a similar position, "The sources of the Nile's inundation are the equatorial rains that fill the White Nile, which originates in east-central Africa (present-day Uganda) and flows sluggishly through swamps in eastern Sudan; and the Blue Nile and the Atbara River, which both fill with melting snow from the mountains and become raging torrents filled with tons of red soil from the basins of both these rivers. The higher the inundation, the deeper the color of red waters. In addition to this discoloration, a type of algae, known as flagellates, comes from the Sudan swamps and Lake Tana along the White Nile, which produces the stench and the deadly fluctuation in the oxygen level of the river that proves to be so fatal to the fish. Such a process, at the command of God, seems to be the case for this first plague rather than any chemical change of the water into red and white corpuscles ... " (*EBC,* vol. 2, 350).

modern historian is able to reconstruct as the event. The meaning of that event takes the place of the meaning of the text.

What has been the outcome or what may be the outcome of this subtle shift among conservative evangelical approaches to the Bible? For my purposes today, I want to highlight one specific result. It has brought about a change in our "cosmic maps." Today, our cosmic maps look more like typical modern secular "cosmic maps" or like typical ancient Near Eastern "cosmic maps." They look less and less like the world we find in the Bible. There has been a gradual, incremental replacement of the meaning of the text and its world by the meaning we have assigned to historical events.

What is the meaning, for example, of Genesis 1 among evangelicals today? For some, the flood geologists, Genesis 1 tells us about a global water canopy. Why? Because the text explicitly talks about it? No. Because that's what flood geologists believe actually happened. For others, Genesis 1 tells us about geological ages. Still, for others, it tells us about the sequence followed by a theistically guided process of evolution. But how much do these views tell us about the author's intent in writing Genesis 1 and the role it plays in the author's overall strategy in the book of Genesis, or the Pentateuch? Our focus is all too often on what we perceive to have happened rather than on what the Scriptures clearly describe.

In the process of focusing on the world that lies outside the text, we have, in fact, focused on our own historically and socially constructed world. Our biblical "cosmic map" is thus being replaced by one which we ourselves are creating. In our world, the Nile does not turn to real blood. In our world the Nile only becomes red, like blood. The Nile becomes red with micro-organisms and the earth was formed through a long period of geological ages. If we are to understand the Bible, it has to fit into that world. Genesis 1 must, therefore, be speaking about long geological ages. Piece by piece and part by part, the biblical world, our "cosmic map," is being dismantled and refitted into another more compatible world. That world is the one we have come to accept as the "real world" of the 20th century.

The greatest threat to our biblical world, however, does not lie in our view of the past but in our view of the future. It has long been held by evangelicals that the message of the prophets is that Jesus is coming again. Some evangelicals have understood the prophets in more realistic terms than others. But evangelicalism has nevertheless preserved the classical biblical view of the world that is heading toward its conclusion. That is, in fact, the blessed hope of the Christian. The return of Christ is the end of the story. Or, as C. S. Lewis would say, the end of the beginning of the story which God will write for eternity. The reality of that blessed hope is directly linked to our acceptance of the biblical world—the biblical "cosmic map." To say it another way, the lack of the reality of that hope in today's world is directly linked to our reluctance to accept the biblical world—the biblical "cosmic map." For there to be an end there must be a beginning. The Bible is the story of that beginning.

This, I think, is what Peter is speaking of when he warns against "scoffers" who will come in the last day. They will say "all things have continued as they were from the beginning of creation" (2 Pet 3:4). In other words, the world does not allow for the acts of God. But Peter's warning is followed by this reminder, "by the word of God the heavens existed long ago ... the world was destroyed by the flood ... and by the same word the heavens and earth that now exist have been stored up for fire" (2 Pet 3:5–7). God is at work in this world. Peter had a biblical cosmic map. The end of the world was going to be like its beginning. God was at work in both. Peter's realistic view of creation led him naturally to a realistic hope of a final redemption.

If we take the biblical world at face value and understand its world to be our own, then our hope should be fixed on our Lord's return. The world had a beginning and it will have an end. Our task is to live in the light of that end. We are to wait expectantly and patiently for His return. That is the blessed hope of every Christian.

# 8

# Johann August Ernesti: The Role of History in Biblical Interpretation

*By John H. Sailhamer*

### Introduction

THIS ARTICLE WILL ADDRESS THE QUESTION regarding the role of history in biblical interpretation.[1] It will do so within the context of an evangelical view of Scripture. By this I mean a view that holds the Bible to be the inspired locus of divine revelation. There are, of course, other approaches to Scripture and hermeneutics. There are probably also other definitions of the evangelical view of Scripture; but I think the view I have described is the classical view that is rooted in classical orthodoxy and the Reformation creeds.

My primary interest in the subject of this article is and has been in the hermeneutics of the OT. The literature and historical situation of the composition of the OT and the NT are different enough to caution against a facile application of the same hermeneutical principles to both. Nevertheless, I believe that the same principles do apply to both, but each in terms of its own specific issues and questions.

In this article I will approach the question of the role of history in biblical interpretation from the point of view of the history of interpretation. I have elsewhere given a lengthy theoretical discussion of the issue.[2] There I argued that history, and especially the discipline of

---

[1] This article originally appeared in *JETS* 44.2 (June 2001): 193–206. Used by permission.

[2] John H. Sailhamer, *Introduction to Old Testament Theology: A Canonical Approach* (Zondervan, 1995).

philology (the study of ancient texts), should play a central role in our understanding about the biblical texts. Who was the author? When was a book written? Why was it written? What is the lexical meaning of its individual words? History also plays a central role in the apologetic task of defending the historical veracity of the biblical record. Are the patriarchal narratives historically reliable? Were the biblical authors influenced by ancient mythology? Did Jesus rise from the dead?

When it comes to the meaning of the biblical text, however, I argued that history, that is, historical reconstructions of the biblical events, cannot, or at least should not, take the place of the depiction of the actual events described in the text.

It is not a question of whether we can accurately fill in the many historical details that have been left out of the biblical picture. I believe we can do that. Our ability to fill out the biblical picture is, in fact, the chief problem. We have the same ability to fill in the historical details of Scripture as we have of painting over the shadows of a Rembrandt painting with intricate details of seventeenth-century life. Our effect on the Rembrandt painting would be no more or less than on the Bible. By filling in the biblical narratives in this way, we may learn much about the events narrated by the biblical writers, but our goal in hermeneutics is not an understanding of those events as such. It is understanding the biblical text. We want to know what the biblical texts say about the events they record. No amount of information from history outside the text will tell us that.

The task of understanding the events themselves is the task of biblical historiography. That, of course, is an extremely important task. It is not, however, the same task as biblical hermeneutics. Hermeneutics, as I understand it, always is and always should be devoted to discovering the meaning of the biblical text. To quote Sternberg, "the text itself has a pattern of meaning."[3]

## History of Interpretation

*1. Introduction*

I now want to turn to the history of biblical interpretation to address

---

3 Meir Sternberg, *Poetics of Biblical Narrative* (Indiana University Press, 1985), 15.

the question of the role of history in biblical hermeneutics. My aim will be to trace the meaning of the phrase "grammatical-historical method." My thesis is that the meaning of these two terms, "grammatical" and "historical," were best defined and defended by Johann August Ernesti.[4] Not only does Ernesti's viewpoint best fit the nature of the biblical texts as such, but his view is also most commensurate with the view of Scripture held by classical orthodoxy and modern evangelicalism.

Ernesti's approach has long been hailed as the definitive statement of what was to be known as the "grammatical-historical method." Many changes have occurred in the meaning of the expression "grammatical-historical method" since Ernesti. Almost all of them make the claim to be the legitimate heirs of Ernesti's method. The most notable change, of course, was the transition to the phrase "historical-critical method." I do not intend to say anything about that transition. Much has been written about that subject,[5] and I do not intend to add to it.

There were, however, more subtle changes in Ernesti's method, and these have come to have a fundamental effect on evangelical hermeneutics. The "grammatical-historical" approach of Ernesti came to the American evangelical world in the nineteenth century by means of the highly successful English translation of Moses Stuart. Stuart had his own ideas about hermeneutical method and about the importance of historical studies in biblical interpretation; and he had a life-long commitment to introduce the American public to the results of recent German criticism. In light of such matters, Stuart's translation of Ernesti offered a highly interpreted version of Ernesti's method to the English world. He did this, as we will see, in both the translation itself and in the notes he copiously supplied along with his translation.

One might say that through Stuart's translation, the "grammatical-historical method" came to be a kind of safe haven from the "historical-critical method." It came to be a way of using the results of some historical methods without committing oneself to the full war-chest of critical tools. It provided a kind of lighthouse to guard against

---

4 *Institutio Interpretis Novi Testamenti* (Leipzig, 1761; editio altera 1765).
5 See especially Hans-Joachim Kraus, *Geschichte der historisch-kritischen Erforschung des Alten Testaments* (Neukirchener, 1969).

venturing too far into the dangerous waters of "historical" science (*Wissenschaft*). There was a feeling of safety in the dark waters of the historical method as long as one could see somewhere on the horizon a clear beacon of light from the text.

This was not, however, the intent of Ernesti's work. It was, in fact, intended to be just the opposite. In his own day, the historical method was already calling biblical scholars, critical and non-critical, away from the text, and it was Ernesti's intent to bring them back solely to the text itself.

To gain a sense of Ernesti's approach, I want to use one of his own basic principles. I want to look at the way he uses two key terms in describing his method. These are the terms "grammatical" and "historical." What did Ernesti mean by these terms? What was the relationship between these terms? In earlier hermeneutical works, the two terms "grammatical" and "historical" were commonly connected by the Latin conjunction *sive*, meaning something like our word "namely." It was "the grammatical, namely, the historical" sense of Scripture that was sought after. When later biblical scholars such as Karl August Keil connected the two terms with a dash or an *et*,[6] it suggested the two terms no longer meant the same thing. It was now "the grammatical and the historical" method.

After a discussion of the background of Ernesti's terms "grammatical" and "historical," I want to give a description of his own specific use of these terms. I will then attempt to show something of the way in which Ernesti's method came to be viewed within American evangelicalism through the eyes of Moses Stuart's translation.[7]

## 2. A Review of the History of the Use of the Terms "Grammatical" and "Historical"

A review of the history of the use of the terms "grammatical" and "historical" in earlier hermeneutical works reveals many subtle shifts in meaning. The phrase "grammatical-historical" was, in fact, coined by

---

6 J. D. Goldhorn, ed., *Keilii opuscula academica ad N.T. interpretationem grammatico-historicam et theologiae christianae origines pertinentia* (Leipzig, 1820).

7 Moses Stuart, *Elements of Interpretation,* translated from the Latin of J. A. Ernesti and accompanied by notes (Andover, 1827).

Karl Augustus Theophilos Keil in his work entitled *Elementa Hermeneutices Novi Testamenti* (translated into Latin by Christoph August Emmerling; Leipzig, 1811). Keil was attempting to update the central thesis of Ernesti that the Bible should be studied like any other book from the ancient past. For Keil that meant the Bible should be studied according to the newly developed historical consciousness introduced by Johann Salomo Semler (1753–1791), a student of the celebrated Sigmund Jakob Baumgarten at the University of Halle in the early eighteenth century.

It was with Baumgarten that, as historian Emanuel Hirsch has argued, "German Protestant theology reached a decisive stage. . . . It went from being a faith based on the Bible to being one based on revelation—a revelation for which the Bible was in reality nothing more than a record once given."[8] It was also with Baumgarten, and his colleague Johann Franz Buddeus (1667–1729), that the concept of "the historical" was given a completely new direction in biblical studies. Before Baumgarten and Buddeus, the notion of "biblical history," which was introduced into the concept of revelation by Johannes Coccejus (1603–1669), was that series of events *recorded in* the Scriptures. Divine revelation was to be found in the events recorded *in Scripture*.

With Baumgarten, and particularly with Buddeus, "biblical history" came to mean that series of events referred to in the Bible. Hence, divine revelation was to be found in the events referred to in Scripture, rather than in the Scriptures themselves. Though subtle, it is not hard to see that such a view represents quite a different view of "biblical history." Recent works on the history of biblical interpretation, such as those of Hans Frei and Hans-Joachim Kraus, maintain that sometime during the eighteenth century a fundamental shift in the meaning of the term "biblical history" swept over Europe. It was a shift in which the meaning of the Bible ceased to be located in the words and sentences of the biblical narratives and came rather to be located in the events and persons referred to by those narratives.

---

8 "Alles in allem darf man wohl sagen: die deutsche evangelische Theologie ist mit Baumgarten in das entscheidende Stadium des Übergangs vom Bibelglauben zu einem Offenbarungsglauben getreten, dem die Bibel im Wesentlichen nichts ist als die nun einmal gegebne Urkunde der Offenbarung." Emanuel Hirsch, *Geschichte der Neuern Evangelischen Theologie*, Vol. 2 (C. Bertelsmann, 1951), 378.

While I am convinced of the basic truthfulness of this oft-rehearsed account of the history of interpretation, I want to look at these same events from another perspective. Most, if not all, accounts of the development of the phrase "grammatical-historical method" are pre-programmed to explain the rise of the "historical-critical method." As important as that is, I want to look at these same events from a more internal perspective. It is rarely noted that most of the people involved in the actual transition were, at least at one time or another, evangelical in their theology. I want thus to ask how this transition affected that part of biblical scholarship that remained evangelical.

In the end, evangelicals during this time opted to retain the phrase "grammatical-historical method" as their distinguishing trademark over against the more negatively charged "historical-critical method." In my opinion, that was largely an apologetic decision. But what effect did such a decision have on the meaning of the phrase itself? The phrase, which was coined to describe a hermeneutic, had come, in fact, to be used as a basis for an apologetic. By the time we arrive at later evangelical expressions of the phrase "grammatical-historical method," the term "historical" had come to mean something quite different than Ernesti intended.

### a. Words and Things

To understand the sense of the phrase "grammatical-historical method," we need to look at two other important terms found throughout the history of interpretation. These are the terms "words" (*verba*) and "things" (*res*). Here I should begin with the observation that up to and including the work of Ernesti, treatises on biblical hermeneutics were written in Latin. This was even long after vernacular languages had begun to be used in biblical studies and theology. Even in the nineteenth century, Keil's work on biblical hermeneutics, which was originally written in German, was translated into Latin. The reason for this is not merely conservatism. The reason was that a long-standing use of certain Latin terms had been maintained in hermeneutical works since the time of Augustine's book *On Christian Doctrine*. Some of these terms have come over into English, such as the "literal sense" (*sensus literalis*) and the "historical sense" (*sensus historicus*). But the two most fundamental terms have, to my knowledge, never been adapted properly into English. These are the terms introduced by Augustine at the beginning of his treatise, "things" (*res*) and "words" (*verba*).

Augustine's basic formula was that "words signify things." "Words" are parts of language; "things" are what "words" point to. Throughout the history of biblical interpretation, the major treatises begin by laying this basic groundwork. Ernesti was no exception. He begins by stating, "corresponding to every word (*verbum*) in Scripture there is an idea or notion of a thing (*res*) which we call the sense (*sensus*)." Meaning (*sensus*) consists of *words* which point to *things*.

It is not an exaggeration to say that the history of Christian biblical interpretation is a history of the attempt to either narrow or expand the meaning of the term "things" (*res*). Augustine, and the medieval scholars who followed him, saw in the relationship of "words" to "things" the possibility of accounting for both a literal and a figurative interpretation of biblical texts. *Words* point to (signify) *things*, but *things* also can point to (signify) other *things*. All *things* get pointed at by *words* (literal sense), but some *things* also point to other *things* (figurative sense). For Augustine, the "wood" which Moses cast into the bitter waters (Exod 15:25) was both a thing which the word "wood" pointed to, and a thing which points to another *thing*, the cross ("wood") of Christ.

Medieval interpretation, both Christian and Jewish, is characterized by establishing links between *words* and *things*, and *things* and other *things*. What often appears to us as a purely arbitrary labeling of words and meanings, is more often than not the result of a carefully drawn matrix of *things* which signify other *things*. The control factor is, obviously, the acceptance of the links between the *things*. In the medieval church that was the role of tradition. It is thus no surprise that the early Protestant treatises on hermeneutics were preoccupied with nailing down the *things* to which the words could refer. Since there could only be a single meaning to the text, any *word* in Scripture could only signify a single *thing*. At the same time, Protestants were concerned to maintain the "spiritual sense" of Scripture, particularly the OT, as it was understood by Jesus and the NT. If the *words* did not seem to point to that "spiritual sense," then it may, or must, be found in the *thing* to which the *words* refer.

The resolution of this problem played itself out in two ways, the Lutheran and the Reformed approaches. Lutherans, such as Glassius, saw every *word* in Scripture as referring either to a *thing* (*res*) or a "mystery" derived from a *thing* (*res*).⁹ The single meaning (*sensus*) of Scripture was identified by Glassius as that which the Holy Spirit intended, either the *thing* or the "mystery." It is especially important here to note that Glassius identified the meaning intended by the *words*, that is the *thing* referred to by the *words*, as "the literal, that is, the historical sense."¹⁰ The literal sense was the historical sense which was the *thing* pointed to by the *word*.

In Reformed hermeneutics the literal meaning (*sensus literalis*) of Scripture lay in the meaning of the *words* (*verba*) of Scripture. Those *words* were either intended in their proper sense, in which case they pointed to *things* (*res*); or they could be taken in a typological sense, in which case they pointed to future spiritual realities (*mysterium*).¹¹ When *words* pointed to *things*, this was simply called "history," or *res gestae*. In Reformed hermeneutics, *things* had no inherent possibilities for meaning. Meaning (*sensus*) resided only in *words*. It was the *words* that rendered *things*, or history, meaningful. What this meant was that meaning, whether literal or spiritual, could only be read off the surface of the biblical text. There could thus be only one meaning, and that was the literal sense, but that literal sense could, and often should, be understood "spiritually."¹²

---

9 "*Ergo praeter sensum literalem, qui ex verbis colligitur, mysticum etiam dari, qui ex rebus ipsis hauritur, negari nulla ratione potest.*" Salomon Glassius, *Philologia Sacra* (Leipzig, 1705 [1623]), 350.

10 "*literam seu historiam*" (350).

11 "*Ubi unicum tantum esse scripturae sensum, eumque literalem, asserit; Et locos illos in quibus praeter historiam, eamque veram & gestam, significatur aliquid futurum typicè, non duos habere sensus, sed unicum, cumque literalem, verum tamen integrum sensum & totum non esse in verbis proprie sumptis, sed partim in typo, partim in re ipsa quae gesta fuit.*" William Whitaker, *Controvers. de. S. Script*, quaest. 5, cap. 2; Bartholomaus Keckermann, "*sensum verbi divini per se tantum umicum esse, eum nimirum, quem intentioni dicentis, & rei significatae natura importat, qui quidem literalis sive grammaticus dici solet,*" both quoted by Andre Rivet, *Isagoge Sev Introduction generalis, ad Scripturam Sacram Veteris & Novi Testamenti* (1627), 214.

12 One can see in this not only how such a hermeneutic (Reformed) provided a firm basis for the typological interpretation that developed in Reformed Orthodoxy in the seventeenth century (Coccejus), but also why questions about the role

In Reformed hermeneutics the meaning of "history" was, and still is in many cases, tied securely to the meaning of the biblical texts. For Lutherans, however, the meaning of Scripture was detachable from *words* and could become resident in the *things* themselves.

Since Ernesti was a devout Lutheran, it is necessary to take a closer look at the Lutheran notion of *things* and *words*. In Lutheran hermeneutics, the *sensus* of Scripture was located either in the *words* or in the *mysterium* pointed to by the things. Meaning (*sensus*) was thus often only indirectly connected to the *words* of Scripture. Though not intended to be so, in this system of interpretation, the *things* of Scripture enjoyed a certain degree of independence from the *words*. Only the literal sense (*sensus literalis*) was securely tied to the *words*.

Consequently, in Lutheran approaches to the Bible, the *things* of Scripture could often become the means whereby, apart from the *words*, outside meaning was introduced into the text. This worked well in allowing a great deal of freedom for christological interpretations of the OT, but there was a price to be paid for such freedom. Allowing christological meaning to reside in the *things* pointed to by *words* opened a door so wide into Scripture that both orthodox scholars and Pietists could import their own doctrines and personal beliefs by truckloads into the text.

By the eighteenth century, the *things* behind the *words* of Scripture were hard, if not impossible, to control by means of the *words* alone. Hence, it was one of Ernesti's primary goals to secure the legitimate control of the *words* of Scripture over the *things* themselves. That was necessary and important for Ernesti, because he genuinely believed that it was the *words* of Scripture, and not the *things*, that were divinely inspired. His basis for that view was the same as all orthodox theology in his day, Paul's statement in 2 Tim 3:16, "All Scripture [*words*] is inspired."

---

of "history" in biblical interpretation have not dogged Reformed hermeneutics quite as much as Lutheran. Another, less charitable, way of putting this is that one can see why classic Reformed theologians often see themselves as taking an historical approach to exegesis when, in reality, they are doing nothing more than retracing the history recorded in the biblical narratives themselves. In my opinion, there is nothing wrong with such an approach as long as one recognizes it for what it is—a textual approach.

In writing his work on biblical hermeneutics, Ernesti was particularly concerned that the meaning (*sensus*) of Scripture was becoming just as vulnerable in the hands of modern historians as it had once been to theologians and Pietists. Historians, too, had gained remarkable access to the *things* of Scripture. Given Lutheranism's stress on *things*, the historian's newly gained knowledge of *things* was quickly being put into service to manipulate the sense of Scripture just as effectively as the orthodox theologians and Pietists had once done.

Therefore, for several reasons—the most important being his concern for verbal inspiration—Ernesti established his first basic rule of interpretation: the meaning (*sensus*) of Scripture could come only through the *words* of Scripture. Regarding that rule, Ernesti said quite clearly, "Entirely deceitful and fallacious is the approach of gathering the sense of words from things. Things, rather, ought to be known from words."[13]

### b. History and Things

From an early period, Protestant biblical scholars had used the term "history" to refer to the *things* pointed to by the *words* of Scripture. That does not mean, however, that they used the term in the same sense we do today. Kraus, in fact, has argued that for Lutheran and Reformed biblical scholars, the biblical "history" (*res*) to which the *words* of Scripture referred was little more than a static system of Christian symbols used in support of orthodox doctrine. Kraus labels this "*Dogmatic Biblicism.*"[14] Two further stages of development of the term "history" or *things* (*res*) were necessary before the notion of *things* came to be seen as problematic for Ernesti.

The first development was the introduction into biblical study of the notion of "time periods," a system of biblical interpretation associated with the name Johannes Coccejus. Coccejus understood the history portrayed in the Bible as itself an actual flow of events, changing with time, and leading to a definite conclusion.[15] Biblical history as such was no longer like a Rembrandt painting that could

---

13 Ernesti, *Institutio*, 13.
14 Sailhamer, *Introduction*, 120.
15 Kraus, *Geschichte*, 21.

be contemplated in its totality. It was now like a motion picture that could be understood only in terms of its temporal sequence. With Coccejus and his school, the *things* to which the biblical *words* referred were forever changed into dynamic, unrepeatable events. They were still the events recorded in Scripture, but they were no longer viewed as verbal events portrayed in *words*. They were more like the ever-changing patterns of a kaleidoscope. One could understand those events only by becoming a part of them and by experiencing them in their own unique moment.

As Kraus has pointed out, it is important to see that for Coccejus, and those after him, biblical history was still *biblical history*. That meant it still consisted only of those *things (res)* to which the words of the Bible referred. The whole of "history" as such was contained within the range of the *words (verba)* of Scripture. Biblical history was not yet submerged into the ocean of world history. World history rather was still viewed within the panorama of the events in the Bible. Moreover, in Coccejus' system, "history" was still controlled by divine providence. It was, in true Reformed fashion, a "history" read off the pages of the Bible itself. There was still no thought of a "history" whose events and meaning could be known apart from the biblical text.

A complete reversal of the view of biblical "history" came about in the early eighteenth century. It came with the Lutheran Franz Buddeus.[16] Buddeus was, of course, still thoroughly orthodox, but he was also the first biblical scholar to approach the events and meaning of biblical "history" independently of the *words* of Scripture.[17] As Buddeus approached the Bible, he took it that what he could say about

---

16 *Historia eccles.* V. Ti (Jennae, 1715, 1719, 1726).

17 "Der Begriff 'oeconomia' wird durch 'historia' ersetzt. Hier dämmert die historische Idee." H-J. Kraus, *Die Biblische Theologie* (Neukirchener, 1983), 24. Buddeus's new understanding of history can be seen in Diestel's description of his major work on biblical history. Buddeus, in very learned comments, enumerated and critically evaluated a large number of viewpoints about the meaning of various events recorded in the Bible. His primary purpose was to explain with the strictest objectivity the events recorded in the Bible and those of the ancient world in terms of the conditions and wider range of events that were true in biblical times. In doing so, says Diestel, Buddeus still understood himself to be explaining the meaning of the text (Ludwig Diestel, *Geschichte des Alten Testamentes in der Christlichen Kirche* [Mauke's, 1869], 463).

the *things* would also be true about the *words* which referred to those things.

In other words, what could legitimately and historically be said about the *things* referred to in the Bible was linked semantically to the words of Scripture. In taking such an approach, Buddeus, of course, reversed the order of meaning. Instead of the *words* giving meaning to the *things*, the *things* were now giving meaning to the *words*. It was at that point, says Kraus, that a genuine historical consciousness had made its way (unconsciously) into orthodox biblical interpretation.

## JOHANN AUGUST ERNESTI

Ernesti's primary goal was to provide an exegetical approach to the NT that was identical to the newly developed philological approach taken in the study of all other ancient literature. Only in that way, Ernesti argued, could NT exegesis free itself from arbitrary interpretation, by which he meant the control of *things*.[18] His basic thesis was that a text could have no other meaning than its grammatical, or historical, sense. That sense, which Ernesti usually called the *literal sense*, is located in individual words. The sense of a word is assigned to the word by "human arrangement and custom."[19] We would call it today "linguistic convention."

That sense consisted of a specific idea, or mental notion, of a *thing*.[20] *Words* assign meaning to *things*. The fact that the *sense* of words is dependent on human custom means that its relationship to *things* is arbitrary.[21] When in a certain language and at a certain time and place, a sense is affixed to a *thing* by a *word*, that *sense* becomes the necessary meaning of the *word*.[22] It is for that reason that

---

18 Gottlob Wilhelm Meyer, *Geschichte der Künste und Wissenschaften*, 5 vols. (Göttingen, 1802–1809).

19 *"Eum sensum verba non habent per se; sunt enim non naturalia aut necessaria rerum signa: sed ab institutione humana et consuetudine, per quam inter verba et ideas rerum copulatio quaedam inducta est"* (Ernesti, Institutio, 9).

20 *"Omini verbo respondere debet, in sacris quidem libris semper et haud dubie respondet, idea seu notio rei, quem sensum dicimus, quod eius rei, quae verbo exprimitur, sensus audiendo verbo instaurari in animo utcumque debet"* (Ernesti, Institutio, 3).

21 "Sed ea (sensus) cum esset ab initio, et institutione, arbitraria" (Ernesti, Institutio, 8)

22 "Semel constituta per consuetudinem facta est necessaria" (Ernesti, Institutio,).

hermeneutics is grounded in historically conditioned situations and hence the *sense* of words must be investigated by means of a proper philological method.[23] That means, the *sense* of the *words* should be discovered from the usage (*usus loquendi*) of the words at the time of the writing of the biblical books.

For Ernesti, the "use of words" (*usus loquendi*) is central to his method. It is just here, in fact, that Ernesti's method clearly distinguished itself from the historical method in his day, and ours. What Ernesti saw as the "historical" dimension of the meaning of a word was the "fact" that at a certain place and time in the past a living human being *recorded* a word in a text in such a way that its usage could be derived by reading that text. A historical moment was preserved, lexically and grammatically, in an ancient text. The historical moment preserved was not the event recorded but rather the recording of the event itself. An event (*res*) had slipped over into a text (*verba*). To discover the meaning (*sense*) of a *word*, one had to look at the *word* in context of other *words* at the time of the recording of an event.

Ernesti was emphatic that to understand the meaning of *words* one should not look at the *things* the words pointed to. The relationship of *words* to *things* was arbitrary and could be discovered only by noting the usage of a *word* at a particular point in time and place. Ernesti believed that different times, places, and settings could radically alter the relationship between *words* and *things*.[24] It is the task of philology to discover the "usage of words" in specific written texts within various historical contexts. That goal remains today the goal of the science of philology.

The hermeneutical aim of the historical method, on the other hand, was, and continues to be, to discover the "sense" of ancient words by reconstructing the world of thought of the ancient writer who used the words. For the historian, the *sense* of *words* is gained from a knowledge of what the *words* are about, that is, it is gained

---

23 Meyer, Vol. V, 494–495.

24 "*Usus autem loquendi multis rebus definitur, tempore, religione, secta et disciplina, vita communi, reipublicae denique constitutione: quae fere efficiunt characterem orationis, qua quisque scriptor tempore quoque usus est. Nam ab iis rebus omnibus vel oritur vel variatur modus verborum usurpandorum: aliterque saepe idem verbum in vita communi, aliter in religione, aliter in scholis Philosphorum dicitur, quae et ipsae non consentiunt satis*" (Ernesti, *Institutio*, 11).

from a knowledge of *things*. Such a historical approach is recognizable from Keil's description of the *"sense"* of Scripture. According to Keil, to know the *sense* of the words of Scripture one must think the same thoughts as the biblical writer when he was writing the book.[25] The meaning, for Keil, is not in the *words* of the author, but in his mind (*mens scriptoris*). To know the mind of the writer is to know the sense of Scripture.[26] It is for this reason that Keil understands the investigation of the sense of words to be an historical task.[27]

For Keil, the investigation of the historical *sense* is a different task than finding the grammatical *sense*. The *sense* of a biblical book must be drawn first from the *words*.[28] The *words* are a necessary help[29] which the writers use for getting their thoughts across to the readers.[30] But knowing the meaning of the *words* is not enough. The *sense* of a book cannot always be known solely from the *words* actually in the text.[31] For Keil, there are also other matters to consider. One must, for example, have a ready command of those *things* which enable us to better grasp the mind of the author.[32]

Ernesti could not have disagreed more with Keil. Ernesti had, in fact, argued just the opposite. Instead of the meaning (*sensus*) of the *words* being derived from *things*, as Keil maintained, Ernesti taught that the meaning of *things* ought to be derived solely from the *words*. Ernesti could not have been more clear on this point. Hear him again: "Altogether deceitful and fallacious is the approach of drawing the

---

25 *"Sensum orationis aut libri cognoscere nihil aliud est, quam iis occupatum eadem cogitare, quae, dum composuit, auctor ipse cogitauit...."* (Keil, *Keilii Opuscula*, 11).

26 *"Quod ubi in quopiam locum habet, is recte scriptoris mentem cepit..."* (Keil, *Keilii Opuscula*, 11).

27 *"Unde patet, indagationem, quae circa sensum orationis aut libri versatur, esse historiam...."* (Keil, *Keilii Opuscula*, 11).

28 *"Hic vero unus librorum N.T. sensus necessario primum e verbis, quae auctores in singulis locis adhibuerunt, cognosci debebit"* (Keil, *Keilii Opuscula*, 13).

29 *"velut adminiculo..."* (Keil, *Keilii Opuscula*, 13).

30 *"His enim, velut adminiculo, illi ad designandas, quas cum lectoribus communicare volebant, notiones et cogitationes usi sunt, neque uti non potuerunt"* (Keil, *Keilii Opuscula*, 13).

31 *"... sensus libri non semper unice e verbis in illo obuiis cognosci potest..."* (Keil, *Keilii Opuscula*, 14).

32 *"ut res quoque eae in promtu sint, quarum est vis aliqua in definienda accuratiusque cognoscenda scriptoris mente"* (Keil, *Keilii Opuscula*, 14).

*sense* of *words* from *things*, since *things*, rather, ought to be known from *words* and their *sense* investigated through legitimate means (philology). For something may be true which is not in the *words*, but that which is to be maintained about the *things* themselves, ought to be understood and judged from the *words* of the Holy Spirit."

It is interesting to compare the note of Moses Stuart on this last point of Ernesti. Stuart says, "By *things*, [Ernesti] means the application of our previous views of things to the words of an author, in order to elicit his meaning, instead of proceeding to our inquiries, in the way of grammaticohistorical exegesis. Not that our previous knowledge of things can never aid us, for it often does so; but that this can serve for nothing more than an assistant to our philological efforts. . . ."[33] It is clear that Stuart completely reverses the point Ernesti has made. Ironically, he does so by suggesting that Ernesti really does not mean what he says. Stuart suggests that what Ernesti really means to say is that we should look at the *things* of Scripture without prejudice. In other words, we should look at them as objective historians. But it is clear that Ernesti does not mean to say that. He means to say exactly what his own words say—that we should not attempt to understand the *words* of Scripture by investigating the *things* they refer to. We can only understand the *things* by looking at what the *words* tell us about those *things*.

Ernesti does acknowledge that sometimes *words* are ambiguous and texts are unclear. In such cases, says Ernesti, *things* can assist an interpreter to "select some one particular meaning." But here, he says, we must use only those *things* which are know to us from the *words* of other texts. "For," he concludes, "when we investigate the sense in any other way than by a grammatical method, we effect nothing more, than to make out a meaning, which in itself perhaps is not absurd, but which lies not in the words, and therefore is not the meaning of the writer."[34] For Ernesti, the *mens scriptoris* is clearly only in the meaning of the words.

---

33 Stuart, *Elements*, 17.

34 "*Itaque res et analogia doctrinae, quam dicunt, hactenus modo prodest in interpretando, ut in verbis vel a multitudine significationis, vel a structura, vel alia qua caussa, ambiguis, ducat nos ad definiendam verborum significationem, sive ad delectum significationis. In quo tamen et ipso cautio est, ut res, quibus ad definiendum*

To show the effect of the later interpretations of Ernesti by Keil and Stuart on American evangelicalism, I want to look briefly at the work by Milton S. Terry, *Biblical Hermeneutics*, a work that continues to enjoy considerable influence among evangelicals today. According to Terry, "The grammatico-historical sense of a writer is such an interpretation of his language as is required by the laws of grammar and the facts of history." For Terry, the historical sense is "that meaning of an author's words which is required by historical considerations. It demands that we consider carefully the time of the author, and the circumstances under which he wrote." Terry then quotes Davidson to show that the two terms, grammatical and historical, "are synonymous."[35]

So far, Terry appears to follow Ernesti fairly closely. Then Terry begins to specify more precisely what he means. Even though the terms grammatical and historical "are synonymous," there is a difference. Where they differ is that the laws of grammar are universal; the special uses of grammar (*usus loquendi*), however, are determined by "the religious, moral, and psychological ideas, under whose influence a language has been formed and molded."[36] Hence, "all the objects with which the writers were conversant, and the relations in which they were placed, are traced out *historically*."[37] It is clear that Terry (and Davidson) have parted company with Ernesti on the crucial issue of the role of history in hermeneutics.

Only a few pages later Terry demonstrates just how much he has learned from the later versions of the "grammatical-historical method" in works such as those by Keil or Stuart. In discussing the importance of "the historical standpoint," Terry says, "The interpreter should, therefore, endeavor to take himself from the present, and to transport himself into the historical position of his author, look through his eyes, note his surroundings, feel with his heart, and catch

---

*utimur, ductae sint ex verbis planis et perspicuis et certo cognitis aliorum locorum, nec adversentur verba, quorum sensum quaerimus. Cum autem aliter, aut per eam solam, sine grammatica ratione, sensus quaeritur, nihil aliud efficitur, nisi, ut sensus repertus in se fortasse non absurdus sit, non ut in verbis lateat, sitque menti scriptoris consentaneus*" (Ernesti, *Institutio*, 13).

35 Milton S. Terry, *Biblical Hermeneutics* (Zondervan, 1974), 203.
36 Terry, *Biblical Hermeneutics*, 204.
37 Terry, *Biblical Hermeneutics*, 204.

his emotion. Herein we note the import of the term grammatico-*historical* interpretation. We are not only to grasp the grammatical import of words and sentences, but also to feel the force and bearing of the historical circumstances which may in any way have affected the writer.... The individuality of the writer, his local surroundings, his wants and desires, his relation to those for whom he wrote, his nationality and theirs, the character of the times when he wrote—all these matters are of the first importance to a thorough interpretation of the several books of Scripture."[38]

What is wrong with what Terry is saying here, in my opinion, is not his hopelessly naïve romanticism. What is wrong is that he presents it as an explication of "the principles so ably set forth by Ernesti [which] were further elaborated ... by Karl Augustus Keil, whose various contributions to biblical hermeneutics [here he refers to the grammatical-historical method] did much to prepare the way for the solid and enduring methods of exegesis which are now generally prevalent in Germany, England, and America."[39] Whether Terry's approach to the use of historical reconstruction is valid in hermeneutics today, I leave to the reader to decide. The point I want to make is that it does not in any way represent the "grammatical-historical method" envisioned by Ernesti.

Let me conclude these remarks on the grammatical-historical method by a brief look at the assessment of Ernesti by the standard work on the history of biblical interpretation in his own lifetime, that of Gottlob Wilhelm Meyer.[40] What one misses most from Ernesti, Meyer says, is any instructions on the use of the historical method. One should, however, not expect to find such instructions in Ernesti because, Meyer asserts, Ernesti relied solely on a grammatical interpretation.[41] Meyer goes on to argue that it was only with Semler

---

38 Terry, *Biblical Hermeneutics*, 231
39 Terry, *Biblical Hermeneutics*, 708.
40 Meyer, *Geschichte*.
41 The full quotation is: "Aber noch mehr vermisste man in dieser Ernestischen Anwerfung, da sie zunächst auf die grammarische Interpretation allein berechnet war, eine Anleitung zur historischen Interpretation . . . und besonders eine Anleitung, die Herablassung Jesus und seiner Apostel zu den nationalen und temporellen Begriffen ihrer Zeitgenossen zu beachten, und aus den Apokryphen des A.T., wie

(independently of Ernesti) that we find an interest in historical interpretation as part of the *sensus literalis*.[42]

## Conclusion

In several of his hermeneutical and philological observations, Ernesti was remarkably ahead of his time. Ernesti, for example, was thoroughly aware of the implications of the fact that the languages of the Bible are dead languages. Such implications have been recognized only recently in biblical studies. In my opinion, there are many valuable and important features of Ernesti's approach, not the least of which is his clear focus on biblical philology over against the historical method.

I have not, however, focused attention on Ernesti because I think we should all follow his hermeneutic today. In looking at Ernesti I have wanted to make only two points. First, what we commonly think of as the "grammatical-historical method" is a far cry from the method of Ernesti. We have, in my opinion, been too quick to link Ernesti with those who later claimed to represent him.[43] The result is that we have come to think of the "grammatical-historical method" as a warrant for the use of all kinds of historical material in biblical interpretation. Ernesti was clear that he believed historical research, that is, historical reconstructions of the events recorded in the Bible, could not and should not be used to inform the text about the meaning of its words. It is the meaning of the words, gained through the study of ancient texts (philology), that is to tell us about the biblical events.

Secondly, I think Ernesti is a good example of how one's view of inspiration can, and perhaps should, effect a hermeneutical method. What characterizes Ernesti's approach more than anything else is the importance he placed on the meaning of the *words* of Scripture. It is true that Ernesti was trained in philology and that he had

---

aus andern lautern Quellen, diese Zeitvorstellungen möglichst genau zu erforschen" (Meyer, *Geschichte*, vol. 5, 499).

42 "... so suchte bald darauf Semler durch ähnliche belehrende Winke neben der grammatischen noch die historische Auslegung des N.T. zu empfehlen, und selbst an seinem Theile zu befördern" (Meyer, *Geschichte*, vol. 5, 501).

43 Note the remark of Gerhard Maier, "Andrerseits wählten Ernesti und seine Schule gerade den Begriff 'grammatisch-historisch,' um ihre Art von Schriftauslegung zu charakterisieren" (*Biblische Hermeneutik* [R. Brockhaus, 1990], 296–297).

a greater appreciation for it than the historical method as such. But the more important factor in Ernesti's approach is the reason why he preferred philology to history in the first place. The reason lay in his understanding of biblical inspiration. Ernesti held to the classical orthodox view of inspiration. The *words* of Scripture were inspired, not the historical events (*things*).

Consequently, the method that best rendered the meaning of the *words* of Scripture was to be preferred. In the annals of the history of the rise of biblical criticism, Ernesti is generally derided for not jumping on board the "history is the answer to everything" bandwagon. But he is also credited with being the last biblical scholar to have held fast to the doctrine of biblical inspiration in the classical sense of identifying inspiration and Scripture. By the beginning of the nineteenth century, the accepted view of inspiration had become focused not on Scripture but on the events (*things*) to which the Scriptures referred. Instead of a "holy Bible," we were given a "holy history." It is therefore no wonder that biblical hermeneutics was eager to make the shift away from the meaning of *words* to the meaning of *things*.

If, today, evangelicalism still makes the claim to believe in an inspired text (*words*), then we would do well to heed the advice of one of our most esteemed biblical philologists. History has an important role to play in telling us *about* the Bible, its authorship, time and place of writing, etc., but when it comes to the meaning (*sensus*) of the Bible itself, there is no substitute for the old-fashioned way—reading the *words* in terms of their grammatical, namely historical sense—as understood originally by Ernesti.

# 9

# Engaging the Disciplines: Selected Book Reviews

*by John H. Sailhamer*

*Review of Gordon Wenham,* Genesis 1–15 *(Word Biblical Commentary; Word Books, 1987), which appears in* Trinity Journal *9.2 (Fall 1998): 231–236.*

WENHAM'S COMMENTARY WILL BE WELCOMED by readers of this Journal as an invaluable *Synopsis Criticorum* of current Pentateuchal studies. His grasp of the issues and bibliography of Genesis is evident throughout and he has exercised considerable judgment in the selection of the material he discusses. Conservative biblical scholars will appreciate his less than positive assessment of the current state of the art in Old Testament studies, though in the development of his own approach to the literary and source critical issues in Genesis, Wenham may engender the suspicion of some. It is clear that Wenham ventures into areas rarely occupied by American conservative scholarship in this century.

His acceptance of J and P material (though not complete documents) in Genesis, for example, will surely be a matter of concern to many conservative readers, even though his assessment of the nature and date of this material differs markedly from that of current critical scholarship and is thoroughly consistent with an early date for the book. An important feature of his commentary that differs greatly from most critical works on Genesis is his focus on the "present form of the text, what Genesis meant to its final editor or author...." Wenham rightly recognizes that "the JEP versions of Abraham's life or the story of creation were known only as they were combined. It is the final text of Genesis that has inspired the faithful down the ages and fueled the imagination of poets and other writers, so it is essential to begin here."

Wenham's view of the source criticism of Genesis is as follows. Wenham identifies with the recent tendency (e.g. Westermann) to eliminate the *E* source in favor of a more simple source analysis. Phenomena such as "doublets" and variation of divine names are explained by means of literary techniques rather than evidence for source analysis. He argues that since the basic outline of Genesis 1–11 follows that of the Atrahasis epic, the plot of these chapters was likely already known in the second millennium BC. "Most of the narratives in Genesis are so vivid and well told that it seems high-handed to deny their substantial unity and split them up into various much less fetching parts" (p. xxxvii). The present text of Genesis, however, is not written on whole cloth, "certain sections stand out as quite different: the genealogies in chaps. 5 and 11 (passages traditionally assigned to *P*) … and when Gen 1–11 is compared with chaps. 12–50, a striking difference emerges.… It therefore looks as though in the pre-literary phase Gen 1–11 had a quite different tradition history from chaps. 12–50. The opening chapters use and modify stories well diffused throughout the ancient world, whereas the patriarchal stories with their focus on the origins of the nations may be presumed to have been passed down within the Israelite tribes" (pp. xxxvii–xxxviii).

Having come to the conclusion that "a number of written and oral sources were used to compile Genesis" (p. xxxviii), Wenham acknowledges that "it is much more difficult to be very specific about where one source ends and another source or editor begins" (p. xxxviii). Wenham thus rejects the common assumption that *J* and *P* are "two continuous written sources in their own right" (p. xxxviii) as well as the more recent view that *P* is a redactional layer in *J*. In his reckoning of the evidence, what is known as P preceded the "major editorial work of *J*." Support for dating P before *J* comes from the fact that whole sections of *P* texts (Gen 5:1–32), according to Wenham, have been edited by *J* comments (Gen 5:29). He concludes, "We therefore believe that the final editor, *J*, had before him an outline of primeval history, an abbreviated version of our present Gen 1–11, which he reworked to give the present form of text" (p. xli).

Was this "outline" the same as what is known now as *P*? No, says Wenham. It is more likely that *J* had before him a "variety of fragmentary sources," some of which were *P* materials (derived from a diversity of sources). Thus his final assessment resembles "a fragmentary and supplementary view of the composition of Genesis while holding onto *J* as the most significant editor of the book" (p. xlii). Wenham dates *J* between 1250 BC, the late date for the exodus, and 950 BC, the earlier consensus on the date of *J*.

It seems that in spirit, at least, Wenham's literary critical approach resembles that of Franz Delitzsch's commentary on Genesis (*A New Commentary on Genesis*, vols. 1 and 2, translated by Sophia Taylor [T&T Clark, 1888]), though in detail there are marked differences. Delitzsch saw *P* (which he called *Q*) as later than either *J* and *E*, whereas Wenham does not recognize *E* and puts *P* earlier than *J*. Both, however, view *P* as the fundamental material lying behind the composition of Genesis and trace its origin back to the earliest stages of Israelite history. Even more importantly, both argue strongly for the unity of the book and the historical trustworthiness of its content. Though I fear Wenham's literary critical assessment of the Genesis text will draw considerable fire from American Evangelicals, it should be acknowledged that this commentary has made considerable strides forward in addressing the literary questions that arise out of the text itself. Especially helpful has been Wenham's ability to view the insights of the current debate in Pentateuchal studies, e.g., the work of Rolf Rendtorff and H-C Schmitt, in a way that produces positive results for the meaning of the text of Genesis as we now have it.

One might have hoped that Wenham would have made an even greater break with the classical literary critical approaches of the past that have fueled such great debates over the historical trustworthiness of Scripture. It is not clear, for example, why he retains the nomenclature of the older documentary hypothesis, JEDP, when he apparently means something quite different by these terms. In any event, Wenham has aptly demonstrated that it is possible to approach the Book of Genesis with a high view of its origin as the Word of God and a true conviction of its historical reliability and at the same time attempt to describe the historical and literary process of its composition. If such concerns can, or indeed must, occupy our attention in dealing with other books of the Bible, e.g., the Gospels, they surely have their place in Genesis as well.

Wenham approaches the theology of the book of Genesis along three lines—its relationship to the mythological structures of the Ancient Orient; the internal relationship of Genesis 1–11 to Genesis 12–50; and the relationship of Genesis 1–11 to modern thought. By far, the greatest attention is given to the question of the relationship of the message of Genesis to its own ancient setting, a setting which Wenham identifies with the mid-second millennium. According to Wenham, "modern man makes assumptions about the world that are completely different from those of the second millennium BC.

Consequently when we read Genesis, we tend to grab hold of points that were of quite peripheral interest to the author of Genesis and we overlook points that are fundamental" (p. xv). Thus, he argues, "an understanding of ancient mythology is essential if we are to appreciate the points Gen 1–11 was making then . . ." (p. xlv). Though there are fundamental similarities between the viewpoint of Genesis and the ancient world ("Indeed Genesis and the ancient Near East probably have more in common with each other than either has with modern secular thought," p. xlvii), the significance of the book of Genesis lies in its polemical stance against the views current in its own day.

Although the ability of Wenham to carry out this plan and relate the message of Genesis to the themes of the ancient world is evident throughout the commentary, it seems to me the hermeneutical pitfalls of such an approach need bearing in mind. For example, in relating the message of the book to a mid-second millennium setting, one runs the risk of not taking seriously enough the role of the book within the final stages of its composition, which on Wenham's reckoning took place at a later time (p. xliv).

The issue I am raising here is not the oft-touted quest for the "canonical context," which Wenham is quite sensitive to. The fact is that Wenham himself appears open to the possibility of a later revision of Genesis and that it was possibly the work of J. He acknowledges that the mid-second millennium cultural setting by which he understands these narratives would not likely have been appreciated in Israel after the 12th century BC. I couldn't agree with him more on this point. One need only read the rehearsal of the Genesis narratives in Nehemiah 9 to get a sense of the remarkably insightful, yet different, way in which those narratives were understood at a later time.

Wenham is right to seek for the original author's intention, but there is need for clarity regarding the point at which one identifies the original author. If the book of Genesis was written in the mid-second millennium, and not merely an early stage of the book, then it seems right to look there for the cultural setting of the narratives. However, if the final authorship is to be assigned to a later period, that would imply a quite different cultural context. In the face of a great deal of uncertainty regarding this later edition, another option would have been to avoid the notion of "authorship" altogether and focus only on the various versions of the material presented in Genesis. Wenham, however, seems to have ruled out such a consideration.

It is unfortunate, as well, that Wenham does not give more attention to the question of how the modern reader of Genesis should relate the content of Gen 1–11 to his own knowledge of the world. Some indication of the direction he would go is his assessment of the genre of the first chapter of Genesis. For Wenham, Genesis 1 "does not stand foursquare with the rest of Genesis, to be interpreted according to precisely the same criteria" (p. 40). Accordingly, Wenham stresses that the narrative of that chapter does not correspond to our world in the same way as the narratives of the rest of the book. It should be read as a "triumphant affirmation of the power and wisdom of God" (p. 40) rather than as an actual description of God's work in six days.

Wenham's point is, of course, appealing to the modern reader but he has not supported it from the text of Genesis 1–11 which is historical narrative and thus we can only assume would have been read with the same expectations as Gen. 12–50. Wenham would like to see Gen 1 at least as "not normal Hebrew prose" (p. 10) or "elevated prose" (p. 10), but he can do so only by pointing to traces of "poetic bicola" in what is admittedly prose material. Nevertheless the issue goes beyond Gen 1 to all of Gen 1–11. Surely the biblical writer, in writing in the *genre* of historical narrative, intended to describe what had, in fact, happened in creation. What Gunkel said already at the beginning of this century still holds good for the intention of the author of chapter 1, "the narrator wanted to say that the regular change of night and day which we see continuously before our own eyes stem from that first day. Moreover, the establishment of the seventh day as a holy day would be superfluous if one does not understand these days as actual days" (Hermann Gunkel, *Genesis übersetzt und erklärt* [V&R, 1977], p. 106).

A further indication of Wenham's assessment of Genesis 1-11 and the modern world is his treatment of the Garden of Eden narratives. Though they are "factual" reports, argues Wenham, they are not "history" as we now know it. Wenham prefers the term "proto-historical" story. As such they do not describe events which actually happened but embody "truths in vivid and memorable form in an absorbing yet highly symbolic story" (p. 55). Wenham here appeals to Gunkel's term "faded myth." There is, however, a problem in an appeal to modern form critical categories to explain the sense of the Genesis narratives in their present state in the book. Gunkel and others have focused on the earlier intentions of the original stories which have been collected in the present shape of the book. It is those stories which they describe as "faded myth" and *Sagen*. But what of their work of collecting and organizing those texts into the narratives that we now have in Genesis? As Gunkel has argued, both the narrators and the hearers of those stories took them to be historically true (*Genesis*, p. xxx). Gunkel says, 'To the narrator these histories were not an embodiment of an idea but dealt with actual realities. It is therefore no little error when modern scholars take the Eden narratives to be an allegory which does not intend to be taken as that which really happened" (*Genesis*, p. xxx).

A feature of Wenham's commentary that many will appreciate is its up-to-date interaction with secondary literature on Genesis. There is, in fact, a healthy balance between interacting with the text itself and with those who have commented on the text. Wenham's own observations and comments on the text show such insight and perception that one wishes more of the commentary contained them. Though such interactions with the latest critical views are unavoidable in commentaries nowadays, it inevitably diminishes their timeless value and narrows the scope of their readership. In any event, Wenham has given us an exemplary balance between the two concerns.

Furthermore, Wenham's grasp of the parallel literature of Babylon, Assyria and Egypt is admirable. It is possible, in fact, to learn a great deal about such works as the Atrahasis epic in reading this commentary. Reading such heavy doses of parallel material, however, makes one yearn for the time when the focus on "the Bible and the ancient Near East," which has so dominated Genesis commentaries in our day, will have run its course. Such concerns will never lose their value as pointers to the historical reliability of Scripture, but measured against the careful and prayerful reading of the Scriptures themselves they seem to contribute so little to our understanding of the biblical narratives.

Here, again, Wenham and the editors of the Word Commentary series have pointed the way in making both aspects of the Bible, its history and its authority as God's Word, the concern of modern evangelical scholarship. There still remains the need, however, to give more regard to the meaning of Genesis within the larger context of biblical theology—particularly the question of Christ in the Old Testament. Wenham appears to work under the common assumption that any christological intention found in Genesis would have to come under the heading of *sensus plenior* and thus could not have been a part of the original author's purpose. Much of this conclusion is a product of his reading the text within the context of early oriental tradition.

On his own reckoning, however, the final editor of the book and much of the material in the book is to be dated later in a time when the earlier context would not have been known. The fact that at a later period in Israel's history there was a much greater concern for themes such as eschatology and messianism would suggest the possibility that those themes may also be at work in final editorial work of Genesis. Even if one were to remain within the context of the parallels in the earliest of the ancient myths, Hugo Gressmann (*Der Messias* [V&R, 1929) long ago demonstrated that the themes of eschatology and messianism were already in the air when these texts were written. Finally, the extent to which the earliest interpretations of Genesis, both before and after the time of Jesus, find messianic themes in these narratives imposes upon the commentator the question of whether such themes were a part of the original author's—that is, final editor's—intention.

For example, the fact that Prov 8:22, Codex Neophyti 1 and Jerusalmi I have read רֵאשִׁית in Gen 1:1 as wisdom (חָכְמָה / חוּכְמָא) and that Prov 30:4 and Neophyti 1 appear to have interpreted רֵאשִׁית as "the Son of God" (ברא דיי) raises the question of whether such an idea was intended by the author of Genesis. Sensitivity to such questions is at least in harmony with Wenham's own helpful maxim: "those closest in time to the composition of Gen 1 may be presumed to be best informed about its meaning" (p. 13).

In any event, it is of no small importance in a theologically oriented commentary to address such issues, especially since this was the meaning read out of the passage by the New Testament writers (John 1:1–3; Col 1:15–18; Heb 1:2) and throughout most of the history of the Church (e.g., Theophilus of Antioch in *Ad Autolycum*, II, 10,13, J.P. Migne, PG, vi, 1023-1168; Augustine, *The City of God Against the Pagan*, Book XI. 22; and Paul Fagius, *Critici Sacri*, Vol 1, p. 4).

*Review of Gordon Wenham,* Story as Torah: Reading the Old Testament Ethically *(T&T Clark, 2000), which appears in* Faith and Mission *21.1 (Fall 2003): 90–92.*

GORDON J. WENHAM HAS WRITTEN EXTENSIVELY on nearly every aspect of the Pentateuch and other parts of the Old Testament. His writings are noted for their thoroughness and insight. He sees things in the text which others have often too quickly overlooked. In this recent book on the narrative nature of biblical "Torah," or, rather, on the Torah nature of biblical narrative, Wenham pursues the question of how ethics might be taught and learned in the biblical narratives of the Old Testament. It has been commonplace to see biblical law as a foundation for ethics, but in this book Wenham asks whether, or perhaps how, ethics might also be the focus of the OT biblical narratives.

Wenham approaches the question by first probing the nature of the OT's understanding of law and ethics, particularly how that is played out in its narratives. How are ethical ideals made manifest in biblical narratives? How are readers expected to distinguish between what literary and narrative characters do and what they should do? How are readers of the Bible expected to emulate its literary characters without sometimes feeling the need to cross their own ethical boundaries? Or, more basically, are readers to emulate the lives of narrative characters at all? Is there an ethical relationship between the biblical narratives and the numerous laws and proverbs in the Old Testament?

For Wenham, the major task of teaching the ethical demands of biblical Torah should be approached from the perspective of the nature of biblical narrative as such. How does one learn anything from the biblical narratives? Are they merely examples of good or bad living? How do we decide? Wenham suggests the task of teaching ethics in biblical narrative has been assigned by the biblical authors to the usual function of literary works, namely narrative techniques, or stratagems. A particularly important stratagem, Wenham argues, is the function of the biblical narrator, or the "implied author." Wenham, in my opinion, is not clear on the distinction of these two literary (or narrative) devices, but he clearly assigns the more importance to the "implied author." The "implied author" is not the author we are used to thinking of as the writer of a biblical book. The "implied author" is the "author" the reader of a book envisions as a kind of conversational partner in and through the reading of the narrative. The narrator, for Wenham, has the task of speaking on behalf of the "implied author."

Influenced heavily by Meir Sternberg's studies of the role of the narrator in biblical Torah, Wenham argues that in the biblical narratives, as in most other narratives, a major part of the process of telling the story of the Bible is assigned to the literary device of narration. Viewing narration as a literary device helps one see that authors, as such, do not directly influence the meaning and ethical values of narrative. Authors make narratives, but narrators and "implied authors" are the mechanisms by which one actually tells the story and moves it along to its conclusion. Authors are usually silent while narrators do all the talking. Narrators also are those who build into their stories the kind of ethical values and principles that become essential, given the role of biblical texts within their communities. The task of teaching and learning ethics from biblical narratives is to keep one's eye on the narrator's way of casting the narrative and the assumptions of the "implied author" passed along to the reader. Ethics are taught by means of such narrative assumptions. If God curses the ground because Adam and Eve disobey him, the assumption is that one should not disobey God's commandments.

Wenham suggests that if we watch carefully the way stories are told and the perspective of those telling the story (narrators and "implied authors"), we will find ample guidelines for interpreting the story in terms of contemporary problems and ethical issues. The task of reading biblical narratives ethically is, then, to identify the author's ethical world as it is reflected in the work of the narrator. It is that world that the biblical narratives mean to impose on their readers. Identifying the author's ethical world amounts to isolating basic narrative techniques in the Bible and identifying the ethical norms signaled and carried along by those techniques.

Wenham confesses there is nothing new in such a process of reading. Jews and Christians have been mining the Bible for its ethical norms for centuries. What is new is the attempt to sort out more consistently or objectively what the readers should take with them from the story and what they should leave behind as part of the story and not that of their own lives.

Wenham makes his case by pursuing a process of close reading of, and drawing broad principles from, two central parts of the biblical narratives, Genesis and Judges. He begins with a discussion of the theoretical aspects of reading and understanding biblical narratives. This he compares with classical forms of literary criticism. The focus of his study is not a critically reconstructed text but the received text as we now have it in the Hebrew Bible. That text, Wenham argues, "is essentially a message from an author to its first readers, which the author hoped would be understood and acted on" (p. 1).

The task of an ethical reading of the OT, says Wenham, is to isolate the various narrative patterns or rules which enabled the ancient readers to follow the lead of the narrator and distinguish good from bad behavioral patterns. In the end, Wenham argues, we are able to see two patterns of behavior exhibited by the biblical characters. In some cases, they follow the morals and models made implicit in the biblical laws. In other cases, biblical characters fall short of those patterns and are depicted in their failure. The task of the reader is to follow the narrator's telling of the story in order to draw the appropriate ethical conclusions. In some narratives the reader is taught the necessity of obedience to the law of God and the corresponding blessing which follows. In other cases the reader is shown that failure leads to the experience of God's grace. So, within the biblical narratives themselves, two essential ethical principles are taught: obedience and grace.

*Review of Joachim Schaper,* Eschatology in the Greek Psalter *(Mohr Siebeck, 1995), which appears in* Journal for the Evangelical Theological Society *42.4 (December 1999): 739–741.*

THIS BOOK REPRESENTS A REVISED VERSION of the author's 1993 Ph.D. dissertation at Cambridge University. Schaper's aim is to contribute to our understanding of the eschatology of early Judaism as a source for NT backgrounds. One must take care to understand this limited focus. This is not a book about the Greek translation of the Psalms as such. It is a book about the influence of Hellenism on Palestinian Judaism in the 2nd century BC. The Greek Psalter is the means for getting us there.

Schaper begins the book by setting it within the context of recent and classical approaches to the Greek translation of the OT. Here his approach is clearly guided by his larger purpose. For Schaper, the focus on the textual history of the Greek Bible and its translation technique, which occupy much of the current study of the LXX, are granted some importance, but center stage is reserved for the study of the historical and cultural context of the translator(s) of the Greek Psalter. Says Schaper, studies of the Greek Bible that focus on linguistic features of its translation vis-à-vis the Hebrew Bible are generally "ahistorical" because they tend to overlook nonlinguistic factors in translation. A word or a phrase might have been translated in a certain way not because of the translator's understanding of the relationship between Hebrew and Greek but because of the translator's dependence on a proto-rabbinical hermeneutic.

Moreover, since we do not have the Hebrew Bible of the Greek translators, it would be anachronistic to suppose the translator used a Hebrew text identical to the present MT. The attempt to reconstruct (through textual criticism) the Hebrew version used by the translator of the Greek Psalter, is "an impossible endeavour." One cannot therefore make absolute statements about the equivalencies of Greek and Hebrew in the Psalms. For that reason, one should focus on the Greek Psalter itself as a religious document in its own right.

Schaper's approach, by his own admission, is reminiscent of earlier scholars such as C. H. Dodd (1935) and Z. Frankel (1851). A major part of Schaper's thesis rests on his dating and locating the translation of the Greek Psalter in 2nd-century BC Palestine. This is also the most tenuous part of his argument. It would be impossible in this brief review to rehearse his justification for this position. In the last analysis, his argument rests on the meaning given to a single Greek word used in the translation and additional corroborating evidence. Schaper himself acknowledges the tenuousness of this argument. Nevertheless the entire subsequent argument of the book is based on this dating and location. Much of the verse-by-verse explication of individual Greek psalms builds on the assumption of a 2nd-century Palestinian origin of the translation.

Before relying too heavily on the results of Schaper's analysis of the Greek psalms one is advised to read carefully the brief chapter on "The Greek Psalms in Jewish Worship" (pp. 131–133). Here Schaper attempts to come to terms with the notion of the use of a Greek translation of the Psalms in the largely Semitic (albeit Hellenistic) context of 2nd-century Palestine. I leave it to the reader to decide whether he has answered all the questions. The bulk of Schaper's study is devoted to a careful and insightful analysis (exegesis) of isolated "eschatological" and "messianic" passages in the Greek Psalms. His general tack in each passage is to show first that the Hebrew passage is best understood non-eschatologically, e.g. Psalm 1 belongs in a wisdom context (Gunkel). The Greek translator, however, saw an occasion in the text to render his own eschatological hope meaningful to his 2nd-century context. It is in those instances where the translator had a measure of linguistic liberty to choose from among several Greek words that we see the theology of 2nd-century BC Judaism of the translator(s) coming through. Here, in just these types of translational opportunities, we can observe the sea-change from OT piety to Hellenistic eschatology and ultimately to Christianity.

The book concludes with three chapters which center on the Greek translator's understanding of the temple and worship in Judaism, the translator's use of early Jewish exegesis, and "Eschatology and Messianism" in the Greek Psalms. It is here that Schaper develops his central thesis: the LXX (that is, the Greek Psalter) is a valuable, but often overlooked, historical source for reconstructing the development of OT religion, through its transformation in Hellenism, to its ultimate rebirth in NT Christianity.

Schaper's study is a bold, and I believe successful, attempt to refocus scholarly attention on an oft-neglected aspect of NT backgrounds. As such it makes a major contribution to our understanding of messianism and early Jewish eschatology. The implications for NT studies are obvious and Schaper does much to bring these to the attention of the reader. There is no need, in my opinion, to pit his own contribution against other quite different approaches to the Greek Bible. The fact that today the LXX is of central importance to serious text-critical work on the Hebrew Bible does not diminish the particular kind of importance Schaper attaches to it.

The Greek Bible offers quite different opportunities when viewed through the eyes of an *Alttestamentler*. Moreover, not all "translation technique" approaches to the Septuagint are "ahistorical," as Schaper contends. In fact, his bibliography and footnotes suggest he has possibly overlooked some translation-technique approaches that, like Schaper himself, do take into account historical and hermeneutical considerations such as proto-rabbinic exegesis and Qumran-type pesher interpretation.

In light of the obvious value of this study, I hesitate to add a criticism. Perhaps it is not so much a criticism as another way to look at the task of using the Greek Bible as an early witness to interpretation. There is, in my opinion, a price to be paid for focusing too heavily on the Greek Psalms as a document in its own right. There is, of course, a place and a justification for doing so, but in a study such as this, I believe it clouds our picture of the role of the Greek translation of the Psalms in the development of Jewish eschatology and messianism in 2nd-century Palestine. In focusing on the sense of the Greek Psalms as such and the context of its translator(s), one may fail to see the equally important historical fact that the translator's own Palestinian community was more a product, not of the Greek Bible, but of the Hebrew Bible, and in particular the Hebrew Psalter.

In my opinion, Schaper's idea of a theologically innovative Greek translator is something of an anachronism. It appears to envision the translator too much in terms of a modern exegete addressing his audience with a theologically new understanding of the Hebrew Bible. As Schaper sees the Greek Psalter, "it served as a means of cultural accommodation to the needs of an increasingly Hellenized Jewish community" (p. 133).

It is also possible to view the Greek translator of the Psalms as someone more intent on preserving the identity of his religious community by means of his translation. What is fundamentally new about the Greek Psalms may only be the translation, not the meaning that is reflected in the translation. Rather than being a new religious document, it is possible that the Greek Psalter was intended to be a document that would conserve cherished ideas that had already made their way into the interpretation of the Hebrew Psalter.

There is, of course, no doubt that many of these ideas already reflected the influence of an emerging Hellenism. But Hellenism did not begin with the use of Greek translations. Part of the problem, as I see it, lies in Schaper's exegetical dependence on earlier form-critical approaches to the Psalms. To be sure, there is little eschatology in an individual psalm once it has been removed from its place in the Hebrew Psalter and set in one of Gunkel's pre-exilic *Sitz im Leben*. As many today have come to realize, though, by the time of the Greek translation of the Psalms, much thought had already been given to the messianic and eschatological implications of the psalms, particularly at the time they were being edited and arranged within the postexilic Hebrew Psalter. By taking such possibilities into consideration one might conclude that the "new" eschatological and messianic ideas in the Greek Psalter were in fact already in the final version of the Hebrew Bible.

This distinction is an important one because on it rests the question of the NT's appropriation of the OT Scriptures. Schaper has ably shown that the NT's understanding of the psalms rests on the shoulders of the Greek translator. The question that remains is how much the translator's own understanding of the psalms draws on the interpretative framework laid down by the framers of the Hebrew Tanak. Had Schaper raised that question, I believe, his results would have been considerably strengthened.

Schaper's work is a welcome and valuable addition to the growing literature on the LXX in general, and the Greek Psalter in particular. He has, to my satisfaction, amply demonstrated his basic thesis that the Greek Psalter represents a kind of eschatological reading of the psalms prevalent in Judaism in 2nd- and 1st-century Palestine and that ultimately fed the hopes of early Christianity. As such he has also shown the importance of the Greek Bible for understanding both early Judaism and Christianity.

*Review of Richard S. Hess and M. Daniel Carroll, eds.,* Israel's Messiah in the Bible and the Dead Sea Scrolls *(Baker, 2003), which appears in* Journal for the Evangelical Theological Society *46.4 (2003): 711–712.*

This book is the publication of the papers delivered at a conference hosted in February 2001 by the Denver Institute for Contextualized Biblical Studies at Denver Seminary. The plan and layout of the book reflect its origin, even to the point of retaining a healthy degree of the usual give and take of such conferences on key issues of biblical theology. The book also reflects the wide spectrum of ideas and approaches represented at the conference. The editors of the book are to be commended for remaining faithful to the conference goals.

The book, as was the conference, is organized around four central papers, each reflecting the topic of "Israel's Messiah" within its varied contexts: in the OT, in the Dead Sea Scrolls, in the NT, and in Latin American theology. One might think of other equally important contexts, but this selection proves well adapted to the topic and purpose of the conference and carries over nicely into the book: There is, in fact, a good deal of the chemistry of the conference itself preserved in the organization of the book. Each of these topics makes its own important contribution. Also contributing to the value of the book as a whole is the apparently conscious decision not to re-edit the papers for publication. For the most part, the papers retain their original colloquial style and collegiality. That spirit of openness, as it turns out, allowed for the airing of a considerable degree of difference between the major papers and their respondents.

In the first section, on the "Messiah in the OT," the main paper is that of Daniel I. Block. After briefly admonishing those who may, in Block's opinion, see too much of the Messiah in the OT for their own good, Block turns to the main point of his paper, the question of how the writers (and original readers) of the OT "perceived" the Messiah when they were, in fact, thinking messianically. Though his point is principally to demonstrate that the Messiah in ancient Israel was chiefly understood as a future (Davidic) king, and not, as many have suggested, also a priest and a prophet, his respondents, J. Daniel

Hays and M. Daniel Carroll R., eagerly take him to task not only on this main point but also on a number of other important issues (mostly hermeneutical) that call into question the importance, if not the legitimacy, of major parts of his argument. One quickly gets the impression that there is still much work to be done on both sides, and, happily, both sides appear to be genuinely listening.

I am tempted to revive here some of the helpful debate represented by the respondents in this first section. But, alas, the reader will have to explore that on his/her own. I cannot move on, however, without calling specific attention to M. Daniel Carroll R.'s one-page discussion on the Servant Songs of Isaiah (pp. 79–80). I found very helpful the way he has framed the issue, and the sense of what he says about it. His (and Daniel Hays's and Karen Jobes's) comments are typical of the high caliber of responses given throughout the book.

The second major section of the book is devoted to Craig A. Evans's paper on the Messiah in the Dead Sea Scrolls. What can I say other than that here one finds a definitive paper on a central topic by one of the leading scholars in the field? The only missing element, which is not unique to this section, is somewhat of a lack of linkage between it and the other sections of the book. Although it is not fair simply to ask for more of a good thing, it can be argued that there is a perceptible missing link between Evans's paper on the Dead Sea Scrolls material and the previous section on the Messiah in the OT. But here we are more likely getting into questions, not about the book and the papers, but about the structure of the conference. It would, for example, have been interesting to have planned a brief response to Evans's paper by the OT presenter. Richard S. Hess, in his response to Evans, wisely alludes to some of this material in the earlier sections, but as it is, the reader is for the most part left to himself/herself to tie together the loose ends.

In some respects the third section, Craig L. Blomberg's excellent and important paper on the "Messiah in the New Testament" is, in the case of this book, a missed opportunity. In his opening paragraph, Blomberg states that a biblical-theological "focus on the distinctive contributions of each NT author or corpus to the varied portrait of Jesus" has "been done repeatedly and accurately" and "requires more than one chapter of a book to accomplish in any detail" (p. 111). He thus decides not to do it but, instead, to "tackle" the specific question of whether the Greek word *Christos* is used in the NT as a proper noun or a title. That is quite a scaling down of objectives! Perhaps this is where the strong hand of an editor could have intervened by insisting he stick to the game plan of the book. In any case his conclusion is important, if still very tentative and of consequence to only a relatively small circle of the book's readership. He finds there is no unambiguous evidence to suggest that any of the 531 occurrences of "Christ" in the NT was ever understood as Jesus' last name. His respondent, William W. Klein, applies equal scrutiny to his own 529 occurrences of "Christ," amicably demonstrating along the way several methodological pitfalls in Blomberg's arguments. Both papers, which are of highest quality, should have been published in a NT journal, rather than in this book.

The fourth and final section, devoted to the Messiah in Latin American theology, consists of a paper by Gerardo A. Alfaro Gonzalez and a response by Karen H. Jobes. Gonzalez's paper is an assessment of the work on Jesus' messianism by the Latin American theologian Jon Sobrino, along with some of his own "hermeneutical observations related to the biblical text and our Latin American reality." Gonzalez's hermeneutical observations (pp. 168–169) are extremely insightful and profoundly stated—and they are applicable not only to Latin America. I found myself reading and rereading his comments in the final two pages of his paper.

I must admit, the title of the book, *Israel's Messiah in the Bible and the Dead Sea Scrolls*, threw me off. It does not tell the real story of what the book is about. But I also have to admit that if the book had been given an appropriate title, something like Messiah in Context, I probably would not have read it and consequently would have missed out on a lively, varied, and insightful discussion. This volume is to be welcomed as one of a growing number of books demonstrating the various ways evangelicals are currently seeking to establish their identity by means of their central theme, Jesus as Messiah. In addition to being a representative example, it is also exemplary.

Much of what is at stake in the broader evangelical position is cast, in this book, in the form of a genuine and insightful dialogue arising out of a sincere desire of the participants to listen and learn from each other. We need more of that. If one were to characterize the volume as a whole, two primary features stand out: (1) the wide variations, not so much in the positions held, as in the approaches recommended for sorting out the details, and (2) the desire and willingness of the participants to listen to each other even though sometimes their criticisms strike home and send them back to the Bible for better answers.

*Review of Hans-Joachim Kraus,* Systematische Theologie im Kontext biblischer Geschichte und Eschatologie *(Neukirchener Verlag, 1983), which appears in* Trinity Journal *6.1 (Spring 1985): 91–94.*

THE PUBLICATION OF *Systematisch Theologie im Kontext biblischer Geschichte und Eschatologie* by Hans-Joachim Kraus is not a surprise to those who have followed Kraus' two-decade quest for a "biblical theology"—one that would treat both the Old Testament and New Testament as theologically relevant. As long ago as the 2nd edition of his *Geschichte der historisch-kritischen Erforschung des Alten Testaments* (1969), Kraus made known his interest in a biblical theology that would close the age-old rift between the testaments (p. 509). His major work, *Die Biblische Theologie: Ihre Geschichte und Problematik* (1970), has as its mainspring the question of whether or not such a "biblical theology" is mere wishful thinking—a "phantom" (p. 1). Those who study Old Testment theology with the same interest in mind are deeply indebted to the work of Kraus, both for that just cited book and in the many articles and monographs devoted to the topic—not to mention his masterful commentary on the Psalms (*Biblischer Kommentar Altes Testament*) which also includes a volume on the *Theologie der Psalmen.* How fortunate now to have in hand an exemplar from Kraus of the "phantom" itself—a systematic theology.

The book is in fact a re-working of an earlier work entitled *Reich Gottes: Reich der Freiheit* published in 1975, and although the present book's content is reflected to a great extent in the title of this former work, the present work is "a completely new" undertaking. The re-working is reflected in the present book's emphasis in its title on "the context of biblical history," which Kraus wants to show is the major contribution of the Old Testament to systematic theology—the historical emphasis on the establishment of the kingdom of God. Such emphasis, Kraus argues, also opens avenues of dialogue between Christian theology and Judaism—a recurring note throughout the present work.

Kraus describes the work as a "textbook" or "workbook" that intends to present "theses" for discussion and attempts to open up systematic theology to the everyday life of the church, the world of business and politics. Following this purpose, the book presents

225 "theses" in its 565 pages of text, along with a general discussion of each thesis and a full "Apparat" at the conclusion of each section. Each one includes a bibliography, notes and further comments on the history of the theological problems. For those accustomed to Kraus' exacting thoroughness and breadth of understanding in his previous works, this book will be found to be no exception. Even when one may not always agree with the direction taken by the author, the present work will be of great value to anyone working with the problems of biblical and systematic theology.

The structure of the book reflects the central concern of the book: to show theology's task as the explication of the historical appearance of the kingdom of the Triune God. Thus, after a somewhat lengthy "Prolegomena," there follow three major sections: (I) "The God of Israel in the Witness of His Coming"; (II) "Jesus Christ in the Proclamation of His Sending"; and (III) "The Holy Spirit in His Work in the Church and the World"—a division that provokes intimations of the threefold task: Old Testament Theology, New Testament Theology and Systematics. Kraus stresses throughout the book the importance of this three-fold division of the book and its sequence. The point of the book's structure is to show that always there is only One God at work, yet always it is the work of the Triune God: Israel's God—Jesus Christ—Holy Spirit. Since, in Kraus's view, it is theology's task to continue in "critical dialogue with traditional dogmatics," as well as to shape itself within the framework of Christian belief (p. v), this Trinitarian schema provides the model and the basis for Kraus's ongoing reorientation towards the doctrines of the early Church.

For example, Kraus argues that the fundamental historicality of the appearance of the kingdom of God rules out the primarily ontological Christology of the early Church councils ("Christology from above") and points to a Christology that must be explained and founded upon the "promise-history" that lies at the basis of the coming kingdom of God (p. 363). Just as the God of Israel is known in history not simply through history (encounter rather than revelation), so we know Jesus "the Christ," not ontologically as the one who always existed, but we know him as the one who was sent, who has come and who will come again. The "vertical doctrine of the Trinity," Kraus argues, must be replaced by one grounded in the "horizontal" movement of "promise-history" (p. 363).

Kraus's emphasis on the reality of the historicality of the kingdom of God also leads him to respond critically to the notion of a "Christology from below"—that is, a Christology grounded in the "historical Jesus." Whatever may be said about the critically assured "minimum" of our understanding of the "historical Jesus," it should not be overlooked that even the kerygma is a part of the real history of the kingdom of God and one's "Christology should be shaped from the totality of the history of Jesus" not just from a "hypothetical and relative" minimum (p. 366). "Indeed, the sending is grounded in an initiative of the God of Israel, in the history of his coming, which begins in the chosen people. This is the 'historical' perspective without which the sending of Jesus, his words or work cannot be understood" (p. 367).

From what has been said it is perhaps clear that Kraus writes his theology very much within the style of dialectical theology. Traditional dogmatics are heard sympathetically and allowed to speak when they are "biblical." More often than not, however, they are censured for their uncritical acceptance of the metaphysics of their day. Modern theologians too are called to account for being too critical and relying too one-sidedly on a rigid historicism. A too-hasty "de-mythologizing" of the New Testament may close one off from an understanding reading of the biblical writers' coded attempts to speak the ineffable. Since it is Kraus's purpose to open lines of discussion, not to close them, the sometimes blurred results of his "theses" cannot be counted as defects, but for one who likes to see issues clearly, the style often proves annoying. But then, the task of theology is often to systematize areas of uncertainty, not merely to explain them away.

In reading Kraus, the question that continually comes to mind is, What is meant by the main thesis that the structure of Systematic Theology is determined by the reality of the biblical proclamation of the coming kingdom? The full impact of the thesis is not always clear. It appears that Kraus means that God has acted in "history" to establish a "kingdom of Freedom," and that it was this kingdom that was the center point of the proclamation of the Old Testament writers. This kingdom was the focus of the preaching of Jesus and the New Testament and it is the plan of God to bring this kingdom to a final consummation at the end of history.

In other words, God's kingdom is just that—one that God Himself will establish. Unlike the Utopian and secular kingdoms of modern liberation theology, it is a kingdom that man cannot bring by himself. It awaits God's continuing act. By the concept "kingdom of God," Kraus means more than the customary "rule of God." He also means the "realm" (p. 17). The insistence on this point leads Kraus into a discussion that would sound very familiar to American evangelicals. The kingdom of Israel's God in the Old Testament has a "this world" component that cannot be overlooked or spiritualized in such a way that the Church takes over all those elements of God's kingdom that once belonged to Israel.

Two further implications arise from this point: first, Kraus is compelled at this point to discuss with some sympathy the concept of a millennium—something not usually taken seriously in modern theology. Secondly, Kraus takes the "this worldly" orientation of the kingdom of God as an occasion at many points throughout the book to enter into a discussion of the political and economic issues in today's world and this leads him to proposals very similar to some forms of liberation theology. Always, however, Kraus stops short and draws a clear line between himself and a theology of revolution because, as he consistently argues, the kingdom of God cannot be identified completely with the present order—the message of the kingdom of God is eschatological. The kingdom of God is a "kingdom of Love" and a "kingdom of Freedom." The final consummation is yet to be and when it comes it will mean that all men will be free. Redemption, reconciliation, salvation—all come to mean freedom for Kraus. As for the inclusion in the kingdom, Kraus appears to take a universal interpretation of 2 Cor 5:19, but appears at the last minute to back away slightly, and conclude ambiguously: "In the power of the unlimited love of God stands the fate of all men" (p. 565).

One further point about Kraus's view of the kingdom of God. The message of the kingdom is a proclamation of a real act of God in establishing His kingdom. In the truest sense of the term the kingdom is "historical." What is its relationship to the "real world" of the modern historian? Since it is a work of God, its "reality" cannot be grasped in the way that "fundamentalists" and "historical critics" want to describe it—as brute facts. Rather, it must be grasped by faith.

From an evangelical perspective it seems hard to side with Kraus on virtually any of the proposals he makes. At the same time, however, the breadth of this work and its mastery of the field make nearly everything he touches one of first importance for further study and of great value to further theological dialogue.

# 10

# Finding Meaning in the Pentateuch: An Interview with Collin Hansen

LATE LAST YEAR, MARK DRISCOLL ANNOUNCED through Facebook the publication of John Sailhamer's *The Meaning of the Pentateuch* (IVP, 2009) with a special appeal to "hardcore uber geek theological types who love footnotes."[1] But his friend and fellow pastor John Piper took issue with Driscoll's suggestion that only a nerdy remnant would appreciate the book.

"To all pastors and serious readers of the Old Testament—geek, uber geek, under geek, no geek—if you graduated from high school and know the word meaning, sell your latest Piper or Driscoll book and buy Sailhamer," Piper blogged. "There is nothing like it. It will rock your world. You will never read the Pentateuch the same again. It is totally readable. You can skip all the footnotes and not miss a beat."

Backed by these endorsements, Sailhamer's 610-page tome on the Bible's first five books briefly broke into the top 100 in Amazon.com's sales rankings. CT editor at large Collin Hansen interviewed Sailhamer, Old Testament professor at Golden Gate Baptist Theological Seminary, about his newest book, biblical criticism, and finding meaning in the text of Scripture.

*How do you explain the meaning of the Pentateuch to evangelicals who revere these foundational books but do not see their relevance?*

---

1 This interview originally appeared in *Christianity Today* (January 11, 2010). Used by permission.

Experience has taught me that we really have to want to understand the meaning of the Pentateuch before we see its relevance for our lives. I've been fortunate to have students who have kept me looking for answers about the meaning and relevance of this book. The old theologians used to speak of "the love for Scripture" as a sign of true faith in Christ. They would say, "We should read the Old Testament as if it were written with the blood of Christ." For them, the Old Testament and the Pentateuch in particular was a Christian book, a book about Christ. For most evangelical Christians today it is a book about archaeology and ancient history.

Here we have to be careful because, to be sure, the Old Testament is about ancient history. But that is not its meaning. Its meaning is Christ. Saying that also calls for a great deal of caution. In my book, I take the view that the whole of the Pentateuch is about Christ, but that doesn't mean that Christ is in the whole Pentateuch. Finding Christ in the Pentateuch means learning to see him when he is there rather than trying to see when he is not there. I like to tell my students that we don't need to spiritualize the Old Testament to find Christ, but we do need to read it with spiritual eyes.

I have a good friend who likes to chide me by saying you don't need "exegesis" to find Christ in the Old Testament. All we need is some "extra Jesus." I wrote my book in part to show my friend and others like him that serious scholarship leads one to find Christ in the Old Testament because he is really there. The author of the Pentateuch put him there when he wrote the book. I've found that if you show someone that Christ is really there in the Pentateuch and the Old Testament, they will come back to "see more," not merely because they have come to revere the Pentateuch as a foundational book, but more importantly because they want to see more of Jesus.

*What is the trickiest problem with discerning the meaning of the Pentateuch?*

The problem can be a simple one. Christians just don't really believe the Old Testament is their Bible in the same way the New Testament is. For them the Old Testament teaches the law and the New Testament the gospel. The Old Testament is about Israel and the New Testament is about the church. They may not say it in so many words, but it's there, especially on those rare occasions when the preacher asks them to turn to an Old Testament passage. For them it's like reading someone else's mail. They feel they need to ask permission to obey its laws. Remember this: What we call the "Old Testament" today was the only "New Testament" Jesus and Paul ever had. All the evangelism we read about in the book of Acts was the result of the gospel they proclaimed from the pages of the "Old Testament."

*How does an understanding of the whole help us understand the smaller parts of the Pentateuch?*

An important goal in understanding a written text is to discover the "intention of the author." Where is he going with his text? Is there a strategy that lies in the author's composition? Such questions help us discover what the author wants to say in both the details and the whole of his text. The author is like a mystery writer who plants seemingly meaningless details for us to discover and ultimately connect to find their meaning. Only when we discover that meaning in terms of its parts and their relationship to the whole can we say we understand the text. Wouldn't you like to see the written notes in the margins of Sherlock Holmes's Bible?

*What can we learn from later biblical figures in how they treated the Pentateuch?*

In my book I have taken a close look at how the later Old Testament authors read and interpreted the Pentateuch. They had essentially the same Pentateuch we have today, plus a number of comments that they passed along as their explanatory notes. Being for the most part prophets, their comments and explanations ultimately found their way into the later versions of the Old Testament text. It is in those notes that we can see most clearly their longing for the coming of a Savior foretold by Moses in the poems of the Pentateuch.

*You argue, "The Pentateuch was written not so much to teach Israel about the Sinai covenant as to teach them about the new covenant." How did you reach this conclusion?*

In reading through the poetic texts that frame the narratives in the Pentateuch, I find they often use the same words and expressions as the biblical prophetic literature. The phrase "in the last days" is a good example. Those same words and phrases carry with them the notion of a new covenant. They are part of the same prophetic composition throughout the Old Testament and were later used by Jesus and the NT writers to interpret the Old Testament. So rather than focusing on the past Sinai Covenant, the Pentateuch is looking forward to a future new covenant "in the last days."

*What one thing would you say to help us change how we read the Pentateuch and how pastors preach from it?*

Keep your eyes on the biblical text. What do their words say to you personally, and what do they tell us about Jesus? Those are the prophetic words that God still speaks to us personally today.

*During your tenure as an Old Testament professor, how has study of the Pentateuch changed?*

By far the biggest change in Old Testament studies over the past four decades has been the fall—if not the total collapse—of the discipline of Old Testament itself. I don't mean to say that the study of the Old Testament has no future. I mean only that there is a general sense among Old Testament scholars at the moment that the discipline of Old Testament studies has an uncertain future. It is not that there is no future. It is that no one has been able to predict what its future will be. This an exciting time and productive period to be studying the Old Testament because despite the many new approaches being tried and tested, a consensus on what will come next has not been reached.

*Several evangelical scholars have recently called on their colleagues to appropriate the methods of critical interpretation. What do you make of this effort?*

I'm saddened by it. Criticism has its place in biblical scholarship, but I cannot envision how or where it would play out in evangelicalism.

As evangelicals we have the responsibility of addressing the questions raised by biblical criticism. But I would expect that to happen alongside of and from within our own "non-critical" perspective.

*What do you expect will be the next great frontier in Old Testament studies?*

The next frontier in Old Testament studies will be the same as its first frontier, that is, the question of the Old Testament's witness to Christ.

# The Writings of John H. Sailhamer: A Comprehensive Bibliography

The following is a comprehensive bibliography of the published works of John H. Sailhamer. In each category, the works are listed in alphabetical order. The entries that have been bolded are the ones found in this volume.

### DISSERTATION

Sailhamer, John Herbert. "The Translational Technique of the Greek Septuagint for the Hebrew Verbs and Participles in Psalms 3–41." PhD diss., University of California at Los Angeles, 1981.

### BOOKS

*Biblical Archeology*. Zondervan Quick Reference Library. Zondervan, 1998.
*Biblical Prophecy*. Zondervan Quick Reference Library. Zondervan, 1998.
*Books of the Bible*. Zondervan Quick Reference Library. Zondervan, 1998.
*Christian Theology*. Zondervan Quick Reference Library. Zondervan, 1998.
*First & Second Chronicles*. Everyman's Bible Commentary. Moody, 1983.

"Genesis." Pages 21–333 in *The Expositor's Bible Commentary: Genesis–Numbers*. Edited by Tremper Longman and David E. Garland. Volume 2. Revised Edition. Zondervan, 2008.

*Genesis Unbound: A Provocative New Look at the Creation Account*. Sisters, OR: Multnomah, 1996. Second Edition. Dawson Media, 2011.

*How We Got the Bible*. Zondervan Quick Reference Library. Zondervan, 1998.

*Introduction to Old Testament Theology: A Canonical Approach*. Zondervan, 1995.

*The Life of Christ*. Zondervan Quick Reference Library. Zondervan, 1998.

*The Meaning of the Pentateuch: Revelation, Composition and Interpretation*. IVP, 2009.

*NIV Compact Bible Commentary*. Zondervan, 1994. Abridged as *NIV Bible Study Commentary*. Zondervan, 2011.

*Old Testament History*. Zondervan Quick Reference Library. Zondervan, 1998.

*The Pentateuch as Narrative: A Biblical-Theological Commentary*. Zondervan, 1992.

*The Translational Technique of the Greek Septuagint for the Hebrew Verbs and Participles in Psalms 3-41*. Studies in Biblical Greek. Volume 2. Peter Lang, 1991.

### Articles and Essays

"1 Chronicles 21:1—A Study in Inter-Biblical Interpretation." *Trinity Journal* 10 (Spring 1989): 33–48.

"2 Samuel 13:1-4 and a Database Approach to the Analysis of Hebrew Narrative." Pages 99–122 in *Bible et Informatique: Interprétation, Herméneutique, Compétence Informatique*. Champion Press, 1992.

"**Archaeology and the Reliability of the Old Testament.**" *Contact* (Winter 05/06): 7–10.

"Biblical Theology and the Composition of the Hebrew Bible." Pages 25–37 in *Biblical Theology: Retrospect and Prospect*. Edited by Scott J. Hafemann. IVP, 2002.

"The Canonical Approach to the OT: Its Effect on Understanding Prophecy." *JETS* 30.3 (September 1987): 307–315.

"Compositional Strategies in the Pentateuch." Pages 272–289 in *Introduction to Old Testament Theology*. Zondervan, 1995.

"Cosmic Maps, Prophecy Charts, and the Hollywood Movie: A Biblical Realist Looks at the Eclipse of Old Testament Narrative." *Criswell Theological Review* 7.2 (1994): 65–81.

"Creation, Genesis 1-11, and the Canon." *Bulletin for Biblical Research* 10.1 (2000): 89–106.

"A Database Approach to the Analysis of Hebrew Narrative." *MAARAV* 5–6 (Spring 1990): 319–335. Also in *Sopher Mahir: Northwest Semitic Studies Presented to Stanislav Segert*. Western Academic Press, 1990.

"Evidence from Isaiah 2." Pages 90–101 in *A Case for Premillennialism: A New Consensus*. Edited by Donald K. Campbell and Jeffrey L. Townsend. Moody, 1992.

"Exegesis of the Old Testament as a Text." Pages 27–96 in *Tribute to Gleason Archer*. Edited by Walter C. Kaiser and Ronald F. Youngblood. Moody, 1986.

"Exegetical Notes: Genesis 1:1–2:4a." *Trinity Journal* 5 (1984): 73–82.

"Genesis." Pages 109–20 in *A Complete Literary Guide to the Bible*. Edited by Leland Ryken and Tremper Longman. Zondervan, 1993.

"The Hermeneutics of Premillennialism." *Faith and Mission* 18.1 (Fall 2000): 96–109.

"Hosea 11:1 and Mathew 2:15." *Westminster Theological Journal* 63 (2001): 87–96.

"Introduction to a New Concordance of the Old Testament." Pages i–xxxii in *A New Concordance of the Old Testament*. Baker, 1989.

**"Johann August Ernesti: The Role of History in Biblical Interpretation."** *Journal of the Evangelical Theological Society* 44.2 (June 2001): 193–206.

**"Reading the Bible as a Text."** Pages 162–165 in *Narrative and Comment: Contributions to Discourse Grammar and Biblical Hebrew presented to Wolfgang Schneider*. Edited by Eep Talstra. Societas Hebraica Amstelodamensis, 1995.

"The Messiah and the Hebrew Bible." *Journal of the Evangelical Theological Society* 44.1 (March 2001): 5–23.

"The Mosaic Law and the Theology of the Pentateuch." *Westminster Theological Journal* 53 (1991): 24–61.

"Preaching from the Prophets." Pages 115–136 in *Preaching the Old Testament*. Edited by Scott M. Gibson. Baker, 2006.

"Walter C. Kaiser, Jr." Pages 375–387 in *Bible Interpreters of the Twentieth Century: A Selection of Evangelical Voices*. Edited by Walter A. Elwell and J. D. Weaver. Baker, 1999.

**"What Have They Done to My Genesis?"** *Christianity Today* (January 6, 1997): 46–47.

"A Wisdom Composition of the Pentateuch?" Pages 15–35 in *Way of Wisdom: Essays in Honor of Bruce Waltke*. Edited by J. I. Packer and Sven K. Soderlund. Zondervan, 2000.

## BOOK REVIEWS

Review of *The Book of Genesis: Chapters 1-17*, by Victor P. Hamilton. In *Hebrew Studies* 33 (1992): 132–135.

**Review of** *Eschatology in the Greek Psalter*, by Joachim Schaper. In *Journal of the Evangelical Theological Society* 42.4 (December 1999): 739–741.

Review of *The Face of Old Testament Studies: A Survey of Contemporary Approaches*, edited by David W. Baker and Bill T. Arnold. In *Faith and Mission* 18.3 (Summer 2001): 110–111.

**Review of** *Genesis 1-15*, by Gordon Wenham. In *Trinity Journal* 9.2 (Fall 1988): 231–236.

**Review of** *Israel's Messiah in the Bible and the Dead Sea Scrolls*, edited by Richard S. Hess and M. Daniel Carroll. In *Journal of the Evangelical Theological Society* 46.4 (December 2003): 711–12.

Review of *Religion in Geschichte und Gegenwart*, edited by Hans Dieter Betz. In *Faith and Mission* 20.1 (Fall 2002): 70–73.

**Review of** *Story as Torah: Reading the Old Testament Ethically*, Gordon Wenham. In *Faith and Mission* 21.1 (Fall 2003): 90–92.

**Review of** *Systematische Theologie im Kontext Biblischer Geschichte und Eschatologie*, by Hans-Joachim Kraus. In *Trinity Journal* 6.1 (Spring 1985): 91–94.

## Papers and Presentations

"A Compositional Approach and Mosaic Authorship." Presented at the Annual Meeting of the Evangelical Theological Society, San Francisco, CA, November 15, 2007.

"Messiah and the Hebrew Bible." Presidential Address presented at the Annual Meeting of the Evangelical Theological Society, Nashville, Tennessee, November 16, 2000.

"**The Nature, Purpose and Tasks of a Theological Seminary.**" Presented at Dallas Theological Seminary, July 2, 1993. Available now in *The Seminary as a Textual Community: Exploring John Sailhamer's Vision for Theological Education*. Edited by Ched Spellman and Jason K. Lee. Fontes Press, 2021.

"The Quest for the Biblical Jesus." Presented at the Annual Meeting of the Evangelical Theological Society, Atlanta, Georgia, November 20, 2003.

## Interviews

"**Finding Meaning in the Pentateuch.**" Interview by Colin Hansen at *Christianity Today* (January 2010).

# Afterword

*Steven A. McKinion*

John Sailhamer joined the faculty of Southeastern in 1999 in the middle of his outstanding career in theological education. I was in my second year as a seminary professor. Traditional graduate-level "biblical studies" as John described it in his presentation to the Dallas Theological Seminary faculty rarely has much in common with my own discipline of Dogmatics. But in countless brown-bag lunches and cross-campus walks with John during our years as colleagues, I found an Old Testament professor whose interests in a theological engagement with Scripture, in ways to read and re-read texts, and in the seminary as a forming and transforming community helped make sense of how Dogmatics relates to ministry. I had never read the paper John presented to the faculty of DTS in 1993, but I did not need to read it; I experienced it. John lived the vision he described, and he never wavered in helping a novice professor learn to live it as well. John's conception for seminary education is as needed today as it was almost thirty years ago when he proposed it.

At the beginning of the current COVID-19 pandemic a pastor friend remarked, "Nothing in seminary prepared me for this." Having taught in a seminary for nearly half of my life, I was taken aback by this claim. Everything I teach my students has prepared them for this moment in ministry. It is true that no classes deal specifically with the question, "What should my church do if a novel virus causes a worldwide pandemic?" But theological education is not meant to simply address the questions currently being asked. Twenty-five years ago, a lecture—not to mention a class—on ministry during a worldwide pandemic would have been mocked. Who would have predicted that a novel virus would cause the entire country to enter a lockdown? Who could have imagined a time when a virus would mean churches could not meet, or at least not meet in person?

Seminaries are not meant to offer specific answers to specifically cultural and historical questions. Instead, theological education—envisioned in Sailhamer's masterful paper that opens this volume—forms the student and the student's mind as preparation for any host of eventualities.

John's focus on the seminary as a text community requires that theological educators remember not only the *significance* of Scripture for ministry, but its *sufficiency* as well. The Bible is the Word of God; it is a text that forms, reforms, and transforms the community of God. It is sufficient for those tasks. The greatest challenges churches, and therefore its ministers, face are textual. What type of person, church, and community does the text of Scripture form? How might one best communicate that message?

Consequently, theological education must be more than the study of that text, or even ways of understanding the meaning of that text, though it is never less than that task. Seminary must train students to engage that text as Christians, within the Christian community. Students do not read the Bible as objective bystanders, but as the people of God. To fully grasp theological education as John described it must mean reading the text as Christians.

Seminary education must be robustly ecclesial, as an expression of its communal core. Ministers will serve real-life churches. Seminary does not train ministers simply for *the Church* but for *a church*, a congregation of real-life men, women, and children who need to be instructed in the Scriptures and led in the worship of the Triune God. In every culture and every age Christians face the same sorts of questions about living and dying; questions of living christianly while paying the bills and navigating challenges. Seminary education prepares ministers for service to and within a congregation of believers who need spiritual nourishment and guidance in godly living. The best preparation for these church communities is first living the text within the seminary community.

Seminary as a textual community shapes ministers to lead churches to be missional communities. The Gospel is a message to all nations of God at work in Christ reconciling the world to himself. Churches have the unique privilege of announcing that message to those who are meant to be the beneficiaries of that work. Knowing the text, understanding the text, and learning to live the text within unlimited contexts and cultures afford churches the opportunity to offer hope to a world that often knows only suffering.

In the day when churches face question of transgenderism, racism, marginalization of faith communities, and even a worldwide pandemic, theological educators cannot lose sight of the fact that their current students are preparing for the challenges of ministry five, ten, and twenty years from now, and not just in the present. The best preparation for ministry in the textual community of the church then comes by the life-shaping work in the textual community of the seminary now.

When John delivered his paper in 1993, no one could have imagined 2020. The major cultural concern of the day was gay marriage, a settled issue in today's world. Imagine telling a student that one day the legendary Bruce Jenner would win a "Woman of the Year" award by *Glamour* magazine. Ministers in churches today face questions few seminary professors could have imagined. Students in seminary today will become ministers tomorrow, and few of us can predict what their world and culture will be like.

Preparation for ministry *within* a textual community (seminary) and *for* a textual community (church) will best shape ministers who, when faced with a generational challenge, will never have to say, "Seminary did not prepare me for this."

# Acknowledgments

As mentioned in the preface, we are grateful to the Sailhamer family for the permission to publish Sailhamer's address on theological education. We are also thankful to several publishers and editors for the permission to reprint material written by Sailhamer originally published in *Criswell Theological Review*, *Journal for the Evangelical Theological Society*, *Christianity Today*, *Contact Magazine*, *Faith and Mission*, *Trinity Journal*, and *Narrative and Comment* (edited by Eep Talstra). We are also grateful for Stephen Dempster (Crandall University) for writing the Foreword and Steven McKinion (Southeastern Baptist Theological Seminary) for writing the Afterword.

# Scripture Index

Genesis
1–11  77, 142, 143, 144, 145, 175
1–15  141, 176
1:1  xvi, 148
1:1–2:4  77–78, 175
5:1–32  142
5:29  142
12–50  142, 144, 145
15:6  xvi
49:1  xvi
Exodus
1:22  116
7:20  116
15:25  127
Numbers
24  xvi
24:7  xvi
Deuteronomy
17:18  25
2 Samuel
13:1–4  174
2 Kings
3:22  117
1 Chronicles
21:1  174
Ezra
7:10–11  25
Psalms
3–41  173
Proverbs
8:22  148
30:4  148
Isaiah
2  175
33:7  114
Jeremiah
36:2  25
Hosea
11:1  175
Joel
3:4  117
Matthew
2:15  175
Luke
24:13–49  xvii
John
1:1–3  148
1 Corinthians
13:12  7
2 Corinthians
5:7  7
5:19  164
Colossians
1:15–18  148
2 Timothy
3:16  129
Hebrews
1:2  148
2 Peter
3:4  120
3:5–7  120

# Person Index

Ainsworth, Henry 116
Albright, William F. 98
Alfaro, Gerardo 159
Allen, Michael 66
Archer, Gleason 175
Arnold, Bill 176
Arndt, Johann 5
Auerbach, Erich 16, 113
Aquinas 113, 115
Augustine 5, 110, 112, 126–128, 148
Ayres, Lewis 70
Baker, David W. 176
Barth, Karl 6, 7, 14, 15
Bartholomew, Craig 71, 76
Baumgarten, Sigmund Jakob 125
Berger, Peter L. 5, 10
Betz, Hans Dieter 176
Block, Daniel 157
Blomberg, Craig 158
Bonhoeffer, Dietrich 71
Braun, Markus 3
Buddeus, Johann Franz 125, 131
Burns, Ken 101
Busch, Eberhard 14
Calvin, John 6, 110, 112
Campbell, Donald K. 47, 48, 175
Carroll, M. Daniel 157, 176
Carson, D. A. 69
Chapman, Stephen 75–76
Cleaver, June and Ward 108
Coccejus, Johannes 114, 125, 130–131
Cross, Frank Moore 12

Dallas Theological Seminary xii, xiii, 15, 32, 47–49, 179
Davison, Ivor J. 64
De Beaugrande 4
Delitzsch, Franz 143
Dempster, Stephen xv, 183
Diestel, Ludwig 131
Dilthey, Wilhelm 18
Dodd, C. H. 152
Dressler, Wolfrang 4
Driscoll, Mark 167
Durkheim, Emile 5
Ebeling, Gerhard 3, 7, 8
Eichrodt, Walter 21
Elwell, Walter A. 176
Emmerling, Christoph August 125
Ernesti, Johann August 121–139, 175
Evans, C. Stephen 71
Evans, Craig 158
Fagius, Paul 148
Farley, Edward 3
Farrer, William 5, 7
Fishbane, Michael 11
Forrest, B. K. 71
Frankel, Z. 152
Frei, Hans 111, 113, 115, 125
Frye, Northrop 13
Gabler, Neal 108
Gadamer, Hans-Georg 5, 10, 55
Garland, David 174
Geiger, Abraham 12
Gibson, Scott 176

Glassius, Salomon   128
Goldhorn, J. D.   124
Goldsworthy, Graeme   67–69
Goodman, Nelson   102
Gressmann, Hugo   147
Griffith, D. W.   109
Gunkel, Hermann   146, 155
Hafemann, Scott   174
Hamilton, Victor   176
Hannah, John D.   48
Hansen, Collin   79, 167, 177
Harnack, Adolf   5, 12
Hays, J. Daniel   158
Heath, Jane   52
Hess, Richard   157, 176
Hiestand, Gerald L.   69
Hirsch, E. D.   55
Hirsch, Emanuel   125
Hitler, Adolf   14
House, Paul   71
Hughes, Howard   107
Idhe, Don   5
Jeffrey, David Lyle   71
Jobes, Karen   158
Kaiser, Walter C.   118, 175, 176
Keckermann, Bartholomaus   128
Keil, C. E.   117, 118
Keil, Karl August   124–125, 133–134, 137
Klein, William   159
Kolb, Robert   70–71
König, Johan Friedrich   6, 9
Kraus, Hans-Joachim   123, 125, 130, 161–165, 176
Lee, Jason   xi, xiv, 47, 177
Lewis, C. S.   94, 120
Lindbeck, George   90, 102–105, 107
Longman, Tremper   174, 175
Lowe, John D.   8
Luthardt, Christoph Ernst   5
Luther, Martin   70–71, 110
Maier, Gerhard   17, 57
Mayer, Louis   109
Mann, Thomas   10
Marsh, William M.   71
McCray, Alden   64

McKinion, Randall   87
McKinion, Steven   xi, 179, 183
Mertz, Fred and Ethel   108
Meyer, Gottlob Wilhelm   132–133, 137
Migne, J. P.   148
Moyers, Bill   76, 83, 85
Pachomius   5
Packer, J. I.   176
Piper, John   69–70, 167
Rambach, J. J.   21
Ratschow, Carl Heinz   6, 9
Rembrandt   122
Rendtorff, Rolf   143
Reventlow, Henning Graf   13
Ricardo, Lucy and Ricky   108
Ricoeur, Paul   5, 7, 18, 20
Ritschl, Albrecht   5
Rivet, Andre   128
Romer, John   13
Ryken, Leland   175
Sailhamer, John   xi, xv, 3, 47, 75, 83, 87, 93, 101, 121, 141, 149, 152, 157, 161, 167, 173, 179, 183
Sailhamer, Patty   xiv, 49, 108
Sanders, James   12
Schaper, Joachim   152–156, 176
Schmidt, Siegfried J.   4, 22
Schmitt, H. C.   143
Schleiermacher, Friedrich   5
Schneider, Wolfgang   87–92, 175
Scholder, Klaus   114–115
Segert, Stanislav   175
Semler, Johann Salomo   125
Soderlund, Sven   176
Spellman, Ched   xii, xiv, 47, 75, 177
Sternberg, Meir   112, 113, 122, 150
Stock, Brian   52
Stuart, Moses   123, 135
Stuhlmacher, Peter   21–22
Swindoll, Chuck   47–49
Talstra, Eep   87, 175, 183
Taylor, Charles   67
Taylor, Sophia   143
Terry, Milton S.   136–137
Tolkien, J. R. R.   94

Towns, E. L. 71
Townsend, Jeffrey 175
Trask, Willard 113
Treier, Daniel J. 67
Trump, Donald xvii
Turretin, Francis 8, 9
Vanhoozer, Kevin J. 10, 52, 66–67
Waltke, Bruce 176
Weaver, J. D. 176
Webster, John 64–66
Wenham, Gordon 141–148, 149–151, 176
Whitaker, William 128
Widengren, Geo 6
Wilk, Florian 52
Wilson, Todd 69
Wright, G. E. 12
Yarbrough, Robert W. 57
Youngblood, Ronald 175